NASTY MEN

NASTY MEN

How to Stop Being Hurt by Them Without Stooping to Their Level

JAY CARTER

CB

CONTEMPORARY
BOOKS

Library of Congress Cataloging-in-Publication Data

Carter, Jay.
    Nasty men : how to stop being hurt by them without stooping to
their level / Jay Carter.
       p.   cm.
    Includes bibliographical references.
    ISBN 0-8092-3794-6
    1. Control (Psychology).   2. Men—Psychology   3. Abusive
men.   4. Interpersonal relations.   I. Title.
BF632.5.C36   1993
158'.2—dc20   93-24317
                                            CIP

Illustrations by Dan Hochstatter

Published by Contemporary Books
A division of NTC/Contemporary Publishing Group, Inc.
4255 West Touhy Avenue, Lincolnwood (Chicago), Illinois 60712-1975 U.S.A.
Copyright © 1993 by James J. Carter
Printed in the United States of America
International Standard Book Number: 0-8092-3794-6
99 00 01 02 03 04 BW 20 19 18 17 16 15 14 13 12 11 10 9 8 7 6 5 4 3

*Dedicated to those butterflies who still
hang out with caterpillars*

Contents

Acknowledgments

I wish to thank my lovely wife, Sheila, for her constant support of my writing and in my life. A dozen red roses, dinner, and finally getting to be alone with me for one night is not enough compensation.

I wish to acknowledge my editor, Stacy Prince, for her undying encouragement, all her hard work, and her dedication to this book.

Thanks to all those people who helped me with *Nasty Men* as readers: Pat Sheuttler, Donna Bickel, Joanne Mikulsky, Sheila Carter, and a multitude of others. Thanks also to the women's shelters in Doylestown, Pennsylvania (Bernadette); New Brunswick, New Jersey (leader of the abuser's group); Reading, Pennsylvania (Women in Crisis); Philadelphia, Pennsylvania; and to the Duluth School of Thought.

Again, thanks to my good friend Barbara Stender for offering a subtitle for the book and an ear for my ideas. Thanks to the men in the Abuser's group in Reading who are decent human beings and who are willing to learn new ways of dealing with their feelings of powerlessness; to my colleagues at the Family Guidance Center in Reading; to the two Johns, the two Jeffs, William, and the other men with whom I learned so much; to Bernadette Crowe; to my friends who encouraged me to write this book: Dave, Duane, Daryl, Andy, Mark, Bob, Randy, and Ron.

A special acknowledgment goes to the 1,500 people who wrote to me after reading my first book, *Nasty People*, and through whom I learned so much. I personally read every letter, even though I could not answer each one.

From the Author

Over the years, women have told me stories of how various men have done them wrong. I've even seen for myself relationships in which the man was clearly a total jerk, and I asked myself why the woman stayed with him. I guess somewhere in the back of my mind I always knew women got more than their fair share of being dumped on, but since I wasn't the kind of guy who did the dumping (I hoped), it didn't really pertain to me.

But after the publication of my first book, *Nasty People* (which told how to deal with invalidators, individuals who try to control and manipulate others), I was astonished by the number of letters I received—mostly from women and mostly about men. At this writing I have received more than a thousand! Along with this, I was elected to the board of directors for a women's shelter. These two experiences made me privy to the indignities that some women had suffered. I realized that women dealing with nasty men have their own set of problems, a set of problems that call for new insights and new strategies. If you are one of the many women trying to live with or get away from a difficult man, or if you're wondering whether or not the man you're with is truly "nasty," I think you'll find this book useful. Maybe you are a man who has this book in your hands because you fear *you* are a nasty man. If so, I acknowledge you.

One of my concerns about writing *Nasty Men* was that I was betraying my fellow men. But when I casually mentioned to a group of my male friends that I'd had many requests to write a book about men, they all thought it was a great idea. "After all," said one of them, "you won't be writing it about *us!*"

Note: All the examples used in this book are based on actual incidents, although I have changed identifying details to protect the privacy of those involved.

1

Understanding the Nasty Man

Most of us (women *and* men) have been hurt, betrayed, degraded, or put down by a nasty person of the male gender. The nasty man in your life may be your lover, your friend, or the husband who swore to love you forever. He may be hurting you big-time (having an affair) or just a little (putting you down), and you feel rotten. We all know at least one person who gets under our skin so much that we fear, hate, or avoid him. Chances are he's the person you were thinking of when you picked up this book.

The most obvious way a guy can hurt you is through violence. He may do something so nasty that it is incomprehensible to you. He may hit you when he drinks. Or he might be unpredictable, suddenly turning on you for no reason, eyes bulging and voice thundering, treating you as if you are the lowest of the low. He may blame you for his rage, and you may have no idea why whatever you did was so awful. You may not even know what you did to provoke him.

Or the man attacks you covertly, chipping away at your self-esteem with insinuations, subtle accusations, or so-called honesty until you feel like a well-chewed piece of gum spat out on a busy highway. This guy can be so subtle that you don't even realize your self-esteem is being taken away from you. He may feel inferior to you (although you might not think so because of his macho act), so he tries to drag you down to the point where you can be controlled by him. You find yourself feeling bad without knowing why. This guy may really care for you, but he is obsessed with control and has to have the upper hand. It's guys like him who put people in mental health facilities . . . looking supportive all the way.

Then there is the predictable jerk, always down or insulting or angry. You know what he is going to do or say, but you can't for the life of you understand why he does or says these things. And as much as you tell yourself he is not going to get to you . . . he does.

What we are really talking about here is *invalidation*. An invalidator treats you a certain way for the express purpose of making you feel less capable or less important than you are. If someone invalidates you at the right time and in the right way, it can make you a psychological invalid (unless you refuse to let him; more on that later).

BEING INVALIDATED

In my last book, *Nasty People*, I examined the process of invalidation in some depth. If you have already read *Nasty People*, you'll find that *Nasty Men* contains fresh ideas and perspectives for dealing with the jerks in your life. Don't worry if you haven't read my first book; this book provides a brief explanation of invalidation. This time around I am using masculine pronouns and perspective. But you should know, women can be expert invalidators, too!

Invalidators have an ability to insidiously undermine your self-esteem, sometimes so subtly that you don't even realize what is happening to you. The invalidator may use what I call a push-pull process, pushing you down when you don't do what he wants and pulling you up when you do. It is similar to dog training, which shows a nasty man's mentality when it comes to manipulating people.

Some men engage in what might be called typical manipulation ("Bring me a beer!"). Others are more extreme. Adolf Hitler was an arch-invalidator. A "Hitler" will do *whatever* it takes to win control over you. His options exceed the options of anyone else because he is willing to go further, even beyond the limits of human decency, to achieve his goals.

It's interesting to note that we keep looking for raving maniacs when we look for evil. We don't look for someone who can write eloquent poetry, be affectionate with dogs, spend time charming grandmothers in homes for the elderly, or carry on a love relationship. We don't look for people like Hitler, who seemed normal to some and did all of these things. We want the evil ones to be ugly, with warts on their faces and evil-sounding voices. We don't want them to be handsome, charming, or fun-loving, as they often are.

The incredible thing about antisocial guys like Hitler is that they don't have a conscious intent to spread evil. These people don't wake up in the morning and say to themselves, "Today, I am going to be really evil." They just don't see beyond their own needs, so they use and abuse others for their own purposes. Unfortunately, the damage they do to others can be irreversible.

Many women do not tell anyone about the mental or physical abuse they are suffering. I know, from letters I have received, that many women live their lives in secret psychological pain from abuse. Millions of women—rich, poor, fat, thin, married, single—suffer. Let me share with you some excerpts from their letters.

I always end up with basically the same partner—very logical, always right, and very argumentative. I have been choosing partners who invalidate me, and I see now that it did start with my mother being invalidated by her father, and so on.

Their sole purpose is to exact from you all your strength. The more care or energy you give them, the stronger and meaner they get. They stalk their prey with false promises, humor, flattery, and finally demands. When you first meet one he seems to care, but as time passes his ways betray him, and you see that his ways only benefit himself.

This person brought up my innermost fears I'd previously confided—and proceeded to throw these confidentialities [confidences] in my face, used them as weapons against me, and remembered everything I said. This person was slowly turning me almost crazy, even telling me I was sick, and all at my lowest time.

I was economically dependent on him. I was so fragile. I stayed for the sake of the children. It was a nightmare.

I confronted him. What followed was the worst, most degrading, most utterly destructive stream of invective I have ever heard. It was totally personal, and it was intended to kill my very soul.

I attracted all the wrong kinds of men. I wanted to please everyone by putting myself in a subordinate position (as Mom had). I ended up working three jobs for him. At times I was reduced to tears and apologizing. I really didn't know what for. . . . He treated me like a princess and a prisoner. I let him take away all my self-esteem. Why do I hurt so? Why do I care? Why do I love this man?

Throughout the book, you'll find other excerpts from letters I've received. I hope they help you see that you are *not* alone.

DEALING WITH AN INVALIDATOR

I can't anticipate all the ways in which your personal Hitler may manifest his control over you. However, I can tell you what makes him tick so you can make some decisions about him, and I can give you some tools for survival. Knowledge about invalidators goes a long way toward avoiding emotional hurt and even physical pain. I can also tell you that invalidation is contagious, so don't be surprised if you nag at your spouse, scream at your kids, or whack your dog with the broom after spending time with your favorite invalidator. Adolf Hitler caused decent people to do terrible things.

If you want to deal with an invalidator, you are going to have to understand him first. Let's start by talking about "putting yourself in another's place" or "walking a mile in another's moccasins." These phrases refer to a thing called *projection*. You *project*, or put yourself in another person's place, so you can figure him or her out. The main problem with projecting is that you naturally put yourself in someone else's shoes . . . as *yourself* (with your own ideas, values, and characteristics). It is a lot more difficult to put yourself in someone else's place . . . as that person. How do you do that? One of the goals of this book is to help you do that. Once the stalked can think like the stalker, she becomes so much safer . . . and so much more dangerous. Let's be dangerous.

THE MOTIVATION

The motivation of an invalidator is power or control or both. He is control-crazy. His obsession with control may come before his ethics, spirituality, and logic (although he may not be above using issues of ethics, spirituality, or logic to strengthen his control). Invalidation may also serve as a release for his hostilities (although it is not a lasting catharsis). I have noticed that invalidators seem to fit into one of three different types.

The Evil One-Percenter or the Antisocial Personality

I call this person evil because his intent is totally selfish; he has no conscience. I call him the one-percenter because most psychology statistics show that one percent of the population is antisocial. It is debatable whether some people are born with a deficient conscience; the theory that severe childhood abuse turns people into antisocial personalities is also debatable. Whatever the reason, some people are evil, and they have left a bunch of good-hearted people agonizing in their trails.

This evil one-percenter sees the whole world in terms of power and control. Any seemingly unselfish thing he does is done for a calculated result. He is a great actor; he can be charming, persuasive, threatening, and terrifying—*whatever* it takes to control. And even though he usually hides it well, his ulterior motive is me, me, me. He actually believes he is better than everyone else.

Typically, he is also brilliant. He knows he needs certain people in order to gain control and win power. He studies people to understand what it takes to control them. He is *compelled* to win. He *has to* be right. The only time he will forgo winning is when he anticipates a bigger win in the future. The feelings of others are important to him only for how they can be manipulated by him for selfish gains. Loyalty, spirituality, dedication, compassion, and love are all seen as weaknesses that he can demand from others and then exploit. He can demonstrate any one of these qualities, but he has the confidence of knowing that he is just imitating them and is not weakened by them.

This guy doesn't mean to hurt you. His invalidation of you is really nothing personal, just the business of his gaining power and control.

The Ten-Percenter or the Difficult Personality

He has been in a close relationship with a one-percenter (his mother, his brother, or a childhood friend, for example) and has picked up many of the manipulative habits of the one-percenter. This person has been so affected by the one-percenter that some or most of his behavior has been learned from the one-percenter. At a very early age he learned to deal with life by copying the one-percenter. He does not have inherently evil intent, but he certainly uses what he has learned to his advantage. He sometimes, even oftentimes, automatically exhibits the invalidating behavior he grew to know.

> "I have been a victim who has chosen to be with an invalidator because I thought I could handle it, and it certainly is getting me down."

The Twenty-Percenter

The twenty-percenter is emotionally emulating a one-percenter or a ten-percenter, but he does not have evil intent. He has been connected to the invalidation, possibly by a distant relative, boss, sibling, teacher, or intimate partner. He has avoided succumbing to totally self-interested behavior and does not exhibit this behavior often, being genuinely remorseful when he does.

THE DISEASE

The tactics of gaining control rub off the one-percenter onto his children, spouse, relatives, or friends. A lot of these tactics (such as verbal abuse, manipulation, physical abuse) are contagious. For example, say your husband was on you all day, insinuating what a lowlife you are. If you go into your bedroom to find that your child has colored the walls you just finished painting, you may take out your hostilities toward your husband on the poor kid (and all he wanted to do was make the walls "pretty" the way you had done the night before).

It is well known that within a family the tendency toward physical abuse (one tactic of invalidation) gets passed down from generation to generation. The pattern is easy to see: The father beats up the child, who is not allowed to vent his anger. The repressed anger builds up throughout the life of the child. After the child grows up, he becomes a father. He is reminded of his experience with his own father, thinks that's how fathers behave, and cannot contain his pent-up rage. He beats *his* kids. Repressed rage is very compelling and sometimes is uncontrollable.

The tendency toward invalidation is not a childhood disease. Adults are prone to getting the invalidator infection also. It spreads in the military from general down to sergeant to private and from spouse to child. It gets passed along insidiously.

A conscious selfish effort by a one-percenter early on in the history of a family may cause family members unconscious control problems for many generations. Then, sooner or later, there may be another one-percenter in the family who takes these mechanisms of invalidation and consciously develops them further. You may enter an argument with this guy in order to try to express your feelings and resolve things. Meanwhile, he is entering the argument *to win*.

"Looking back, although I felt sorry for him—I always felt bad when with him. The problem now is that I find myself making some of the same remarks to our two boys as he does [invalidating them]. When I do it to my babies, I feel so bad. I feel so much hate towards him that we are at the point of no return."

The next chapter, called "Misunderstandings," will help you differentiate between the kind of nasty behavior we're talking about here and the plain, everyday differences that men and women are prone to have. In Chapter 3, we'll begin to get into "types" of nasty men and how to deal with them.

2

Misunderstandings

Before we dissect your favorite jerk, I want to discuss some general misunderstandings that men and women seem to have. I've placed this short chapter *before* any serious discussion of nasty men because I think it's important for you to know that just because your partner does not agree with you all the time does not make him nasty. You can have disagreements and arguments without his being the kind of nasty guy this book is about.

Men and women are different. Some differences are wonderful and exciting, but some of them make living together difficult. Some problems arise from issues that could crop up between *any* two people—one of you likes Mediterranean-style furniture, for example, and the other prefers French provincial. But many differences are gender-specific. Chances are, he was raised to think and act one way, you another. It is no wonder that you misunderstand each other now and then.

Misunderstandings are the major cause of war and divorce. A misunderstanding occurs when you both think you understand but you really don't. We are all familiar with the type of situation in which there are two people from different countries trying to communicate. One is trying to say that the other is a fine-looking person, but the words are mispronounced, and the other person thinks she heard "fine-looking cow." You and your man are, in many ways, speaking different languages because you were raised differently and so have different perspectives on things. Love, for instance, is not the same thing to a man that it is to a woman. Sex is not the same thing. (Don't forget, I am generalizing here. Certainly there exist a male and a female somewhere who agree on what love and sex are. Let's hope they meet one another!)

This chapter, on misunderstanding, is extremely important; it will help you distinguish between misunderstanding and actual nastiness. Nasty behavior usually stems from the intent to hurt or the lack of intent not to hurt. In other words, some people like to hurt others, and some people don't care if they hurt others as long as they get what they want. In *People of the Lie*, M. Scott Peck says that a person who doesn't want to know that what he does hurts others is an evil person. A man who is willing to know and grow, who does not intend to hurt, and who listens to his conscience is a decent man.

It is valuable to know the common misunderstandings that *do not* reflect ill intent.

DIFFERENT FRAMES OF REFERENCE

Men and women are raised differently and therefore have different frames of reference. (There are also differences between men's and women's biological frames of reference. For example, a man can never experience, and thus never fully understand, what it is to give birth.) Deborah Tannen, in her excellent book *You Just Don't Understand*, says that women and men are "enculturated" differently. Men are raised to be independent, while women are raised to nurture relationships. Typically, if a boy is having trouble starting the lawn mower, he doesn't get help until he reaches the point where he just can't do it. If a girl is having trouble, her dad runs right out and helps her. A girl learns how to get help via her relationships, and a boy learns to figure things out himself. A woman is not afraid to ask for help or admit that she needs it. A man may be ashamed of needing help.

Most men have been raised to produce results (earning money, for example) with little regard for people or ideas not directly related to the results. They are, in effect, taught to have tunnel vision, to focus on a goal and go for it. In football, when someone is in your way you plow through him to get to the goalposts. And football is a apt metaphor for the way many men run their lives. Women, however, are raised to put people before goals. After all, you might hurt someone if you knock him down. A woman's concern for another person supersedes the goal of getting a silly ball across a field.

This difference can cause conflict in a family. A husband, for example, focuses on a goal and if someone gets in his way, he proceeds anyway. A male bystander (say a son or father) who gets in the way is likely to dust the footprints off his back and not take it personally, or at least to understand that the goal had to be reached. If it is a woman (say a wife or mother) who is in the way, she is usually very upset. "My God! There are footprints on my back! I can't believe that the SOB could just ignore me [or blow me off] like that!" If a man is working on a project, he may do *anything* to get his wife to leave him alone so that he can complete it. Later he just shakes his head, unable to understand why his wife is so upset over a couple of footprints.

Let's say a man is rushing around the house, trying to accomplish all the things on his to-do list, and his wife decides to give him a hug (perhaps because she is appreciative that he is finally doing something around the house). Though he loves her, he is in "goal mode" and may somewhat resent being interrupted. He is likely to stop long enough to give her a token greeting, but his wheels are still spinning. The longer she delays him from accomplishing his tasks, the more frustrated he feels. She thinks he is blowing her off and wants him to stop and acknowledge her more meaningfully. He may get very upset at this point and pull away from her, thinking to himself, "Does she want me to do these things or not?" She'll probably say something about how he doesn't pay attention to her, and he begins to wonder if he can ever satisfy her.

Now let's say the wife is going about *her* task, and the husband decides to give *her* a hug. Most likely, she will hug him back and enjoy it. She is good at switching gears and knows she'll be able to get back to her tasks once the more important relationship need is met. Even if she really wants to get back to what she was doing, she'll move around the person obstacle diplomatically. She may not finish as fast, but she is able to nurture her relationship with her husband along the way, so things go more smoothly.

When the husband does his chores the following week, it is unlikely that he will get any help or understanding from his wife; she remembers the last time he was in goal mode. But last week's discord doesn't change the way he approaches her today; he is, after all, doing these things for *her*.

FEELINGS ABOUT FEELINGS

A woman, not wanting to be a nag, will often put up with her partner's goal-oriented behavior (which might include ignoring her feelings). She will think about how she can make things better, talk to friends, and read books like this one. But rarely will she try to have "relationship" talks with him for fear of angering him. So for her, the relationship is operating at somewhere around 55 percent capacity, but he thinks everything is fine and at 100 percent, and then . . .

The Last Straw: A Man's View

One morning the man and the wife leave for work. As usual, she is behaving like a sweet, angelic, supportive wife who thinks the world of her husband. When they get home that night, he is face-to-face with a demonic being who lists all of his shortcomings in one vile breath. This is very perplexing to him. He tries to think of what he may have done to cause this change in his wife's behavior, but actually nothing has happened between them during the day. This woman says the most horrible things to him. She screams about his leaving his socks on the floor (which didn't seem to bother her before), and his solution (men always move to solutions instead of dealing with feelings) is to promise to pick up his socks (for God's sake). He is a little unnerved by her explosion over such a thing. Why didn't she tell him it bothered her before?

Since a man's primary mode of communication is through words, he is listening to what she says without noticing her feelings. He therefore doesn't acknowledge them, which upsets her even more. Instead, he distances himself from her, treating her as if there is something wrong with her. (She interprets his distancing and his logical tone to mean he is cold and uncaring. She turns from upset to angry to livid.)

The Last Straw: A Woman's View

After being taken for granted by her partner, a woman might decide (once again) not to put up with it anymore. Something (perhaps a conversation or a newspaper article) has reminded her that she deserves better. She deserves a real relationship, complete with deep conversations and intimacy. Now, all the valid complaints she has been holding in come out forcefully. She feels it is *his* fault that she has been holding it all in. She knows he doesn't like to talk about this stuff, but now she is so upset that she is not going to give him a choice.

She is sick of him watching TV, sick of him running off to play tennis every weekend, sick of him not bothering to call her when he's working late, and sick of him being engrossed in his projects. It comes down to acts of omission: he omits acknowledging her feelings and omits spending time with her. She feels like one big omission! And the next time he ignores her, she is going to trip him as he flies by!

A little acknowledgment of each other's feelings will go a long way toward solving these problems. As he is doing one of his "fly-bys," it wouldn't take much effort for him to give her a little kiss or hug or tug. And it would be much better if, when he is in goal mode, she greeted him quickly and verbally ("You sure are getting a lot done today, honey!"). If he is *always* in goal mode, then it is time for her to sit down with him and get him to agree to set aside a portion of the day to spend together. He can add it to his daily schedule.

Since men are raised to value action more than feelings, they may actually show their feelings (affection, for example) through their actions instead of words. A woman may be feeling unacknowledged while a man is saying to himself, "Jeez! I fold the clothes. I pick up my socks. I take out the garbage. I work overtime to pay for the car. I finished everything she had on the list for me to do. What else can I *do*?" Of course, what she wants most of all is to have her feelings acknowledged.

Life would be a lot easier for a man if he could get the idea into his head that he doesn't necessarily have to *do* anything to make his woman happy. If that is true of your partner, tell him.

COMMUNICATION

A woman is trained by culture to know her feelings and to develop her intuition. She is usually comfortable initiating conversation and experiencing a meaningful exchange. On the other hand, a man does not like to think about, much less discuss, feelings, and he considers a session of sports talk to be a meaningful exchange. He is less animated than usual when forced to talk about feelings.

When a woman is interacting with another woman, she notices the feelings of the other person more than a man would. If a woman says, "I don't know how I'm going to pay all my bills this month," the other woman might say, "I know what you mean. This month was a rough one for me, too." She shows empathy but is careful not to say anything that could be taken as judgmental or insulting. A man's response might be "Well, I have an extra fifty bucks I could lend you." He is trained in problem solving: If something bothers you, let's eliminate the source of it. He is not judging the woman, nor is he empathizing. He is offering a solution, but without acknowledging any feelings.

Or consider this example: a woman may complain about her job but also be willing and able to tolerate it. She is dealing with it by blowing off emotional steam on a regular basis. The man who hears her complain about her job week after week will wonder why the hell she just doesn't get another job.

From a very early age, a man is taught to downplay his feelings. He tries not to let his feelings get in the way of reaching his goals. In one way this is good, because it enables him to go after his goals unimpeded. *Because* he is able to set aside his feelings, a good man can be counted on to do the "logically" right thing, no matter how scary, and keep his composure about it. But in another way, a man's denial of his feelings is bad, because he can get so far out of touch with his feelings that he doesn't know what he wants emotionally or who he is. He may not even know when something bothers him. Sometimes, an observant, sensitive woman can know what a man's feelings are even when he doesn't know himself. This can be of great value to him (whether he knows it or not).

A woman can forgive harsh words much more readily than a man can. From her frame of reference, words are not that significant anyway, unless they are *meant*, which means they are substantiated with feelings and follow-through. She knows that people say things they don't mean; she has said things she didn't mean. To a man, words are rich in meaning. Words get burned into his brain. A man's self-esteem is greatly affected by what he thinks his partner thinks of him. Much of his self-image is formed by what his loved one says of him, and it is very confusing for him to hear two different characterizations of himself on two different days. He doesn't notice the feelings of his partner on either one of those days and focuses only on the words. Because of his dimness where feelings are concerned, he has to be prompted, "Please just listen. I am going to tell you my feelings. This is important to me, but I don't expect you to *do* anything about it." By the same token, women have to take care not to "take over" a man's feelings; when he finally does open up, she needs to listen and not just assume she always knows more than he does about himself.

MOTIVATIONS

Arguably, the highest priority for a man is the desire to achieve independence. Secondarily, he may be motivated by the need for intimacy or relationships.

Arguably, the most important thing to a woman is the need for intimacy in relationships, with the need for independence taking second place.

When a woman asks a man to pick up some dog food on his way home, she is just mentioning a task that needs attending to. A man may take the request to be a demand made in order for her to wield control over him. He will then unconsciously and conveniently forget to pick up the dog food, or he will do it when he pleases and not when she wants him to. However, if she presents the task as a problem of hers ("Oh, darn! We're almost out of dog food"), then he might be more inclined to solve the problem. If, on the other hand, *he* is the one to ask *her* to pick it up, she is usually grateful that the practical aspect of the relationship is functioning smoothly.

Because a man is goal-oriented, he thinks the arrival is more important than the trip. He doesn't stop to smell the roses; he doesn't think that is important. He is lucky that women exist, because it is through women that most men experience joy. It is the woman who persuades a man to stop and have a picnic along the way. He may grumble that they are not going to make good time, but he ends up relaxing and relieving the stress of the trip. He enjoys himself in spite of himself.

When a man becomes a Zen master, he is enlightened. He realizes that joy and pleasure in life come from everyday acts as well as from great ones. The *way there* is just as important as the destination. Just think of all the time a man must spend studying to be a Zen master to learn what most women already know!

SEX AND ROMANCE

Take a boy and raise him to get to the bottom of things, to achieve a goal and move on, to push those barriers out of the way and go for it. Make him strong. Train, "enculturate," and peer-pressure him to deny his feelings, endure pain without wincing, and score that touchdown. What kind of sexual relationships do you think he will be ready for when he reaches manhood?

Men are not trained to make the feelings of others a priority. In high school, some boys drive their cars past girls and yell out to them, "Yo, babe! Wanna go for a ride?!" They actually think that this will turn on a girl so much that she will say, "Wow! What a stud. Come on over here, big guy!"

Most young males begin their sexual careers in goal mode. They want to "get it." Their fantasies are of the ultimate act. Young women are more concerned with the chase, the lure, the relationship. Their sexual fantasies are about the romance, the aesthetics, and the feelings.

These two different frames of reference can wreak a lasting havoc in relationships between the sexes. She is a tease. He wants only one thing. She realizes that he didn't take her out to dinner because he enjoys her company. He had a goal in mind! He thinks she is just trying to drive him crazy, leading him on and then turning him down. Both may end up feeling rejected and used.

Irreconcilable? Maybe not. Most people know what is romantic to a woman, but what is romantic to a man? A man's idea of a romantic time might be sharing some of *his* interests with her and having her enjoy them. He might be in seventh heaven sitting on the couch, with her beside him, sharing pizza and watching the latest version of *Robocop* on video. He might like to have her keep him company and help him with some of the mundane things he does. He'd enjoy having her help him wash the car or go with him to pick up some things at the hardware store.

But just because your man does not want to cuddle during the Super Bowl does not mean he is nasty. It may just mean that he can't cuddle and be excited about the game at the same time. And if he yells for you to please bring him a beer, it could just be that he doesn't want to miss a play on his way to the refrigerator.

Now that you have an understanding of difficult behavior that is *not* nasty, let's move on to the kinds of guys who give men a bad name. If your man is *always* watching TV, *demands* you bring him a beer, and *never* acknowledges you. ... With some effort from you and some confrontation by you, the rest of this book can help you get him back to cuddling up in front of the fireplace (or at least it will help you light a fire under his butt).

3

Nasty Men

Can you kiss a frog and turn him into a prince? If your guy is a Don Juan, an invalidator, an abuser, or just plain ignorant, you may be wondering if you can change him. Can Beauty transform the Beast in real life? Maybe the true love of a dedicated woman *can* change an abusive Beast into a gentle, flower-picking creature. But if a woman has a Beast whom she cannot change, perhaps she can change her *relationship* with him.

Yes, there are princes out there ready-made. But perhaps they're boring or not very mysterious. Another problem with a prince is that he can have his pick of women. Besides, it's romantic to find a frog and work for his princehood. He'll be oh, so grateful, too. If your thinking is like this, you may realize (if you're now involved with a nasty man) that these ideas are just illusions. Being with a nasty man can be hard on anyone, but especially on a woman who loves him. Nasty men have a habit of being nastiest to those who love them most, probably because they know they can get away with it.

In this chapter, I have spread the many traits of nasty men over several different characterizations: the Verbal Batterer, the Don Juan, the Liar, the Cro-Magnon Man (the generic bastard), and finally the Physical Batterer. No matter how much these generalizations seem to match someone you know, you must remember that we are not talking about real people. Your jerk may be a jerk only with you. Or he may be a jerk with most people, but there is someone with whom he is different. (Maybe he's nice to his mom? . . . dog? . . . car?) He may seem so bad that he is the epitome of the word *loser*. Try to remember that he is a human being.

It is very important that you read about each of the men in this chapter. Even if you don't think your man is a Don Juan, the character discussed in the Don Juan section probably shares some qualities with your nasty man. Each chapter also contains tips for dealing with the nasty behavior specific to each character. You'll find general strategies for change in the last section of the book along with other ideas that are useful for handling all nasty men.

THE VERBAL BATTERER

I have received so many letters about this guy that it almost seems as if there is one Verbal Batterer whose personality has been cloned over and over again in different parts of the world.

The Verbal Batterer makes use of a smorgasbord of invalidation techniques. He can embarrass you in front of your friends and family, making you feel like zero. As soon as you feel the least bit good about yourself, he knocks it out of you. He's likely to remind you of your shortcomings and then blame you for all the trouble you have supposedly caused him. If he is somewhat intelligent, he can rationalize his behavior and twist events in such a way that your family and friends believe him when he bad-mouths you, and maybe even *you* believe him. He is convincing and forceful and righteous. The lower your self-esteem gets, the more you believe him and the more you are in his control. He works hard at having something "on" you, like a past indiscretion that he blows out of proportion or financial dependence or children. He feels threatened unless you succumb to his will. He punishes you in many subtle and some not-so-subtle ways when he believes you have stepped out of line. When you resist, he escalates his abuse. He seems to know what really gets to you. He looks for things that you are ashamed of and sticks your nose in them, constantly trying to make you believe that you are a lower form of life.

> "My daughter has been married to him for twenty-five years. He has a little tiny egotistical mind. She has been supporting him for all these years, not just financially but building up his morale and so on, while he makes her feel tiny and wrong all the time. He constantly puts her down."

Believe it or not, the damage the Verbal Batterer causes can be worse than the damage caused by the Physical Batterer: to ruin someone's mental health can be more damaging than giving her a black eye. Sometimes, however, verbal battering comes with physical battering. They are not mutually exclusive.

PROJECTION

Suppose your spouse comes home and accuses you of cheating on him. Many of us would feel guilty because we all, at one time or another, have been attracted to persons other than our spouses. You might question yourself and wonder if he was picking up that kind of vibration from you. You would probably start to *introvert* (become hyperself-conscious and self-blamingly introspective) about what you might have done to deserve the accusation.

In reality, it is often those who accuse others of wrongdoing who are guilty—in thought, word, or deed—of the very

thing they are accusing others of. This unfair accusation—
the accuser suspects or blames someone else for actions he
himself has taken (or wants to take)—is called *projection*.
You can learn a lot about others by noting their projections.
If your spouse accuses you of cheating and you have not
cheated, then maybe you should check out your spouse
instead of introverting about it. Has *he* been cheating on *you*
in thought, word, or deed?

Listen to the projections of others. It will tell you a lot
about *them*.

JUDGMENTAL GENERALIZATIONS

> "He is either totally withdrawn and glued to the TV or
> viciously pointing out my flaws. I am a Pollyanna type,
> replete with an ulcer and migraines."

Your child uses a nasty word. The invalidator says, "What
kind of a mother are you, anyway?" He attacks your self-
esteem instead of dealing with the real problem. What does
he mean, exactly? (He is letting your imagination fill in the
worst possible details.) How do you approach the problem
of being a bad mother? These are vague issues to attack.
Presumably, if the child cleaned up his language, your
mothering ability would magically increase.

Some kinds of judgmental generalizations are easy to
spot: "You're a bitch" or "You're a lousy cook" or "You're
dumb." Watch out for the ones that are more "believable."

A judgment is only a judgment. I could make up fifty of
them right now; so what?! It has nothing to do with the
price of eggs or your worth. Please know that I am not
merely blowing you smoke; an inaccurate generalization
really doesn't have anything to do with your ability or worth.
The next time he says something like "Why did you let the

kid have a cookie?" just tell him, "Because I'm a bad mother!"

The invalidator's judgmental generalizations are usually made in an attempt to manipulate you. When you hear one, take heed, and look *out there* instead of at yourself.

Hint: Taking It Personally

Here is a mistake: taking people's behavior toward you personally when you needn't. A clerk at the store has just hung up the telephone on her boyfriend after having a big fight. Then you come along, and she throws your change at you. What do you do? Some of us would ignore the act and then think about it resentfully later. Others would take it as a personal attack and get into it with the clerk.

Someone who didn't take it personally would view the situation for what it was. Perhaps she would say, "Having a bad day?" or "The next time you throw my change at me, I'm speaking to your manager." This person wouldn't leave the store with anything left over and wouldn't introvert about something in her own past. If you feel yourself over-reacting to someone's behavior, stop and ask yourself, How much of this is from the current moment, and how much is from the past?

If the store clerk treats you badly (just as your older sister did when you were kids) and you feel yourself wanting to jump over the counter and pummel the little pompous ass . . . perhaps you are overreacting.

You shouldn't let comments from people who don't even know you upset you. Their behavior so obviously says nothing about you, but something about them. I don't mean for you to use the idea that you should not take things personally as a rationalization for these kinds of invalidation. I mean it as the simple truth, because once you truly see it, people's poor treatment of you ceases to have the same effect.

Even if someone says something derogatory about you that is absolutely true, it may still not be necessary that you take it personally. First, it has to be established that the person knows you well enough to make the statement. Even then, the intent of the person has to be established. Is he saying it to help you? If not, then he must be saying it to cause some effect on you, and then the statement is irrelevant even if it is true. There are plenty of things about any human being I know that I could dig up and chastise him or her for. Why? To control this person? To get some attention off of myself? Because I am jealous? Because I'm in a bad mood? To get revenge for something I think this person did to me? There are a thousand possibilities. If someone does not have the decency to approach you in a friendly manner, you don't have to entertain his problem, be friendly, or introvert about his possible reasons. OK? *You don't have to take it personally*. It is that simple.

MANIPULATION

Invalidators are manipulators by definition. They are takers. There are a thousand ways to manipulate and con people. Persuasion, threats to embarrass you, insults, insinuations, and false compliments are all verbal methods of manipulation.

Manipulation is a word we use to mean "bad control." "Good control" is aboveboard and ethical. It involves free will and fair exchange. For example, you pay the kid next door after he mows your lawn. Sometimes good people feel they are being manipulative when they are forced to behave in a secretive manner, hiding things from their nasty men. Sometimes it is hard to stick to your ethics in an unfair situation. The unethical people seem to have more options open to them because they are capable of doing things that you could not ethically do.

If, for example, someone is threatening to hurt you, is it unethical for you to con the person into a position where you can tie him or her up against his or her will? If someone is going to shoot you, is it unethical to take the person's life? It is not within most people's typical behavior or ethics to shoot anyone, even with good reason, because most people simply could not conceive of someone shooting *them*. They say things to themselves like "Oh, he wouldn't actually shoot me." Because *their* ethics would simply not allow them to kill someone else, they naively assume that another human being could not kill them. It's not that they don't think they're in danger—it's that they can't believe such evil exists.

The fact that you believe something (that your husband would never play around, for example) does not make it true. (Furthermore, the fact that *he* believes it does not make it true.) This is how a demonic leader can get away with mass suicide or mass extermination. Would I deceive Hitler, lie to Hitler, or shoot Hitler to protect myself or others? Yes, I would.

One problem we have is that everyone has done something that could be called manipulation. Let's be very clear about something. It is not the *act* that is manipulative, it is the *intent*. If a woman is married to a very suppressive, alcoholic, unethical, or wife-beating man . . . and she fools him into signing over the bank account so she can leave with the

children in the middle of the night . . . is that being manipulative? I think that she is just exerting good control and
showing good sense and good judgment given the situation,
as long as her intent is not to hurt her husband, not for
selfish gain. Now, if she persuaded a good, trusting man to
get drunk so she could run off with his best friend for the
evening, that would be manipulation.

The key is *intent*.

Building You Up and Cutting You Down

Building you up and then cutting you down is a ploy by the
nasty man to make you dependent on him for your self-
esteem. It usually starts off with you being the most wonderful person in his eyes. For a while, you can do no wrong.
Once he has you hooked by setting himself up as the source
of your self-esteem (which you have let him become), he can
manipulate you by pulling out the rug whenever he wants.

Never depend on someone else for your self-esteem. He
may not have your best interests at heart. If you do, he can
keep you from feeling good about yourself unless you are
doing what *he* thinks you should be doing. You are the
captain of your soul and you should be doing what *you* think
you should be doing.

Yes, building you up and cutting you down is very manipulative of him, but it is *your* problem. You are looking for
your self-esteem in the wrong place. If he can manipulate
you in this way, it is only because you have let him. Shame
on you. And speaking of shame, get rid of that too.

The Double Bind

A friend of mine was living with a man who had confided to
her that he had a hard time making a commitment because
he was afraid he would be abandoned. In a moment of love
and compassion, the woman told him that she would never
abandon him. Later on in the relationship, she was miserable

because of all the invalidation he threw her way. He was moody and took out his moods on her. When she would say she couldn't stand it anymore, he would say he was sorry, and he would promise not to do it again. He would beg her not to abandon him, reminding her of her promise.

This was an awful predicament. It seemed that no matter what she did, the outcome would be negative. Blaming herself did not solve it; only awareness did. Let me explain. Right now, you are reading this book. You are reading the words in this very sentence and your attention is probably focused on it. You are probably not noticing your posture or the colors or sounds around you.

Take a few seconds, and put this book down, stop thinking about it, and notice your surroundings. Yes, now. I said, *now*. Really do it!

Good. I don't want you to be introverting (thinking, thinking, thinking) as you read this book right now. Remember when you were a child and you could smell smells and feel feelings, and you didn't have that little voice in the back of your head. Yes, that's right. *That* little voice. The one that just said, "What little voice? I don't hear any little voice." *That* one.

From your first year of school, you have been taught to think, think, think (introvert, introvert, introvert). Some problems cannot be solved through thinking/introverting. When you are sitting there introverting, the world is small. So many times we get stuck there in the limited space of our own frames of reference.

The first part of the answer to the double bind is to stop introverting, get a bird's-eye view, "pop out of yourself," and look at the whole situation. How many different ways can I say it? *Look*, don't *think*.

OK, now let's see how this woman's dilemma was solved. It seemed wrong for her to leave the man after promising him she wouldn't abandon him. But it was an intolerable situation for her to stay in. She couldn't leave without breaking her word, and she couldn't both stay and keep her sanity.

At some point, she stopped introverting over it and looked at the whole picture. What she saw was that (1) it was *his* problem, yet he put the responsibility for it onto her (typical of double binds); (2) it wasn't just a promise at stake, but her sanity; and (3) his intention was to control her.

She told him the following: She wasn't going to abandon him, but she was going to move out. He had promised her he would stop invalidating her, and he had broken that promise. The issue was *invalidation*, not abandonment. She would see a counselor with him (so as not to abandon him) if he wanted to work on *his* problem. Furthermore, she was going to cut off their communication whenever he put her down.

He became angry and said, "If you don't stay here with me, I am just going to figure you abandoned me." She said, "I have already made my decision, and I have no control over what you think."

He went to counseling with her but did not continue after a few sessions. She broke off with him but continues to talk with him as long as he doesn't invalidate her. Their relationship has become a friendship. He now says that she is the only woman who has ever stuck by him.

The whole solution to a double bind is to get out of its trap. It is usually a logic trap, one that keeps you introverting. Your own paradigm, or frame of reference, is what inhibits your finding a solution. Very often, it helps to tell another person about the dilemma. He or she may have a frame of reference different from your own and might see past your limited logic.

Of course, the woman could have avoided getting into this double bind. She should never have promised not to abandon the man. She was trying to fix his problem. That's a nice thought, but people have to fix their own problems. Anything else is just a crutch that keeps the one with the problem stuck. Contrary to popular belief, love and compassion don't fix problems; they only provide an environment for growth.

DOUBLE MESSAGES

Your invalidator says in a sarcastic tone, "You are home a little late from class tonight, aren't you, *hon*?!" After you get defensive and tell him you had a flat tire, he backs off and says endearingly, "You don't have to explain to me. I trust you." Sure, he does.

Whenever you get a double message, address both messages. "Yes, I am a little late. What's with the tone of voice?" When he denies that his tone was accusatory, pin him down. It is all right for him to have his little insecurities, but he has no right to inflict them on you. If he wants to talk about his insecurities, it would be big of you to be supportive. But if he wants to discuss how wrong you are for being late from class, turn the tables. Get the attention off yourself and back to the source of the problem.

One woman, named Barb, wrote me that she worked in a lab at night, alone with a man named Roger. In the beginning he had made sexual advances to her, and she had turned

him down. The previous lab technician had reported him for
sexually harassing her. After that he was sure to say only the
proper things, but he said them in a derogatory, covertly
sexual tone. Barb was intimidated by him and loathed going
to work because of him. One night he greeted her with "You
look lovely tonight," in a guttural tone, as he lewdly stared
at her. Barb said sarcastically, "Why thank you, Roger."
Then she walked over to him, looked him in the eye, and
said, "And by the way, Roger, screw you." It worked. He
never messed with Barb again, and he treated her with
respect. Later she met Roger's mother, who was an extremely dominating woman. Evidently, Roger harbored hostility for women and didn't like them all that much, but he
was capable of respecting them.

One of my little reserve tactics, if I can't think of anything
to say to a Verbal Batterer's comment in five seconds, is to
ask the invalidator to repeat what he or she said. Depending
on how it was said, I change my tone of voice. If I want to
seem mad, I grit my teeth and say, "*What* did you say?!" If
I want to appear coy, I act overly friendly and look at the
Verbal Batterer closely so I can see him or her do it again.
"What did you say (twinkle, twinkle)?" The invalidator
doesn't usually repeat the remark the way he or she said it
the first time.

WHY ARE YOU BEING INVALIDATED?

There are three major factors that predispose people to
becoming victims of Verbal Batterers.

1. Submission Conditioning

All children are conditioned to respond to a certain tone of
voice, expression on someone's face, or a physical gesture.
Since society has, until recently, seemed to demand a great
amount of submission from women, girls were taught to
read these signals and to respond to them with submission.

Some adults react to these cues with submissive behavior, usually without realizing it.

2. Low Self-Esteem

People who are verbally battered often believe they are powerless, bad, stupid, or some other such thing that someone said about them. Adult verbal abuse sufferers are likely to have had their negative sides highlighted and their positive sides ignored or belittled in childhood.

3. Narcissism

Anyone raised by abusive parents probably has an exaggerated sense of her impact on the emotions of others. Though not self-centered in the true sense, these people were raised to believe, and still do believe, that they *cause*, and therefore *are responsible for*, other people's feelings. Dad or Mom may have said things like "You ruined my day," "You are making me miserable," "Look what you did to me," or (a projection) "Stop being so selfish," and their children get the idea that they have control over the emotional state of others.

The net result of these three major factors is that a verbally abused woman is usually introverted and defensive rather than objective and responsible. In other words, she gets into someone else's mind-set instead of forming her own. Having her *own* thoughts and behaving the way she wants to behave is something she would typically have learned to do in adolescence or young adulthood. Some people learn it later, and some people never learn it.

The amazing thing about learning to think and act for yourself as an adult is that it's not a long, protracted process, the way it is for most teenagers. When you're an adult, as soon as you *realize* that you're your own person, you can just start acting like it. It takes some practice, of course, but most adults lack the ambivalence that prevents teenagers from making the transition smoothly. Once adults realize they have this basic, human right, they can just go to it. (If you feel you need help in this area, the last chapter of the book will help give you the confidence you need.)

TIPS FOR HANDLING VERBAL INVALIDATION

- Always, always, always pop out. Never, never, never introvert when you are getting a verbal battering. This is one of the most important techniques you need to put an end to abuse. (All other tips supplement this most important one.)
- Pay attention to your feelings. If you feel like someone just took a shot at you, he probably did.
- Try not to take it personally. If you feel you can't help but do so, ask yourself how much of your reaction is to the present situation and how much of it is to garbage from the past. This is tough at first, but like any other skill that has to be learned, you will get better at it.
- Acknowledge the feelings of the invalidator. He may just be upset with you but not good at expressing his feelings. If you are in a generous mood, you may be able to get him to express himself and put an end to the invalidation. For example: "Gosh. You must be angry with me. Have I done something to make you angry?" He may then feel like he can open up to you with his real feelings because you will listen without attacking him.
- The *cause-effect* response is usually effective when logical attempts to combat verbal abuse have failed. Once I saw a husband following his wife around the house, verbally abusing her. She walked into the kitchen and over to the refrigerator with him following close by. She took out an egg, turned to him, and smashed it against his forehead. They both ended up laughing. He realized he was out of control, and it made *him* stop the behavior.

  Another man complained to his wife one evening, outlining all her faults. He told her he was just being honest.

Then he went to sleep. She ended up staying awake until one o'clock in the morning introverting about all her faults. But after she popped out, she realized that he had pointed out *many* faults, and that he had ruined her rest like this many times before. She went outside, brought in the water hose, and stuck it down the sleeping man's pajama bottoms. Then she went back outside, turned on the water, and enjoyed his screams of anguish. She came back in laughing and told him that from now on, he'd better make sure he kept her in a good mood before bedtime, or it would happen again. She told him that if he had any complaints about her that he could tell her *one* thing that bothered him, after dinner and at no other time.

- If things are out of control, shelve the conversation temporarily. If you find yourself being verbally abused, or verbally abusing someone else, nothing is going to be resolved at that moment. It is best to cool off for a while, think of an approach, and try to resolve things later.

- Approach a man rationally. When a woman approaches a man with a quiet, reasoned appeal, he will almost always take it seriously. If you start mixing in emotions, you may lose him, because he may have a hard time separating the feeling statements from the reasoning statements. If he starts verbally abusing you, you may say something like, "What is your purpose for saying *that* to me? Are you trying to resolve things, or are you trying to hurt me?" You may have to repeat it until he becomes rational again. If he doesn't become rational again, then wait until later and say something like "Yesterday, I was trying to get us to resolve an issue we have, and we couldn't resolve it. I don't think you were trying to resolve it at all. I think you were trying to hurt me, and now I feel like a fool." He may apologize or at least acknowledge your plight. If he doesn't and he starts the abuse again, then tell him what *you* are going to do to resolve the issue, unless he really wants to discuss it rationally. Stand your ground and don't get into an argument. Repeat it only once: "I have told you what I am going to do. You can try to hurt me, but you are not going to bully me into changing my mind." If he has to win and prove his control, then you have a bigger problem than can be handled with words. You may want to consider some serious changes in your relationship (these are spelled out later in this book).

THE FINE ART OF THE REASONED RESPONSE

I don't want to suggest that there are standard answers to verbal abuse. Each situation is different, and people are different. It is important for you to act in ways that fit your personality and ethics as well as the situation at hand. But I know it can be helpful to have examples of what works, so I have included a few sample responses to some different kinds of verbal abuse. Please remember this is not a dialogue for you to follow—just words that have been effective for other women.

He Says	Typical Responses	Better Responses
"What the hell are you doing?"	Cringe. "Shut up!" "I'm sorry."	"Are you upset about something?" "I am picking up the papers you have left strewn across the floor for the last three days, just as I said I would."
His eyes bulge. He raises his clenched fists in the air. "Never touch my papers! Do you hear me? Never."	"This place looks like a sewer, thanks to you." "What am I supposed to do?"	(Humorously) "Then *never* leave your papers out for three days." "Please don't talk to me in that tone of voice."

He Says	Typical Responses	Better Responses
		"Your eyes are red, your fists are clenched, and you are shouting at me."
"Uh-oh! Buckle your seat belts: Mary's driving!"	Tries to be a good sport and play along with the "joke." "You want to drive? Here, you drive."	"If you have a problem with my driving, please don't joke about it. We can talk about it rationally later." "It makes me nervous when you watch my driving so closely and criticize me—and then I *do* drive badly. Please be quiet so I can relax and drive well."
"What's the matter? Can't you take a joke?"	"That's not *funny!*" "Sorry."	"You know I can take a *joke*, but that didn't seem like a joke to me." "I don't enjoy jokes that are at my expense."
"Don't get so upset!"	"Well, then you tell me how upset I *should* get, O Master of the Universe." "Shouldn't I be upset?" "You want to see upset? I haven't even begun!"	"Please don't try to tell me how to feel." "Does my getting upset bother you?"

He Says	Typical Responses	Better Responses
"Is it that time of the month?"	Cry. "Screw you!"	(In a rational tone of voice) "I am making a valid point. Please don't change the subject." "If you are truly concerned with how I feel, I appreciate it. I feel fine. Now what were we saying?"

ONE LAST THOUGHT

Say your child is carrying a glass of grape juice across your new carpet, and you get hyper and say something like "Be careful with that! Don't spill it on the carpet!" That will increase the chances of having it happen. It's like saying don't think about elephants.

I remember a colleague of mine who was judgmental even though he was not the boss, and who constantly criticized others when talking to me (so I knew he criticized me when talking to others). He was a perfectionist and expected flawless performance from his peers. When his subordinates would inform him of a problem, he would always second-guess them and interrogate them as if to suggest that it was *their* fault the problem existed. He had such a strong expectation that people would mess up that he actually made it happen. When I was in this man's presence, I could feel his eyes burning through the back of my head and sense his superior attitude. I also made many mistakes. I got caught up in his life drama, so to speak.

Then, one day, I found a mistake *he* had made. When he came in, I acted just the way he did when he found a problem. I interrogated him and questioned him. After putting up a couple of good defenses, he became very confused and disoriented. After a time, he said, "Who are you? My father?" Then I realized where he had learned this behavior. I said, "No, Joe, but I thought I would give you a taste of your own medicine. You know, I can go all day without making a mistake, but as soon as you come on the scene, I screw up royally. I feel like you are watching me and it makes me self-conscious." We had an hour-long conversation, and Joe wasn't as intense with me after that. Evidently, his father had acted that way toward him and Joe had performed his tasks better because of it. I told him that that didn't work for me: I would respond better with positive acknowledgment and didn't feel it was his place as my peer to monitor my performance. We became good friends.

Why should you bear the burden of someone else's invalidation? *Demand* respect, not just for yourself, but for the one who is disrespecting you. He *needs* to respect you, for *his* own good! You are not being nice or doing anyone any favors by letting him treat you badly. Get out there and *kick ass*!

THE DON JUAN

Love, more than any other single thing in this world, gets mixed with illusion. The Don Juan takes advantage of this. If you can learn to discriminate between illusions and love, you will have gained wisdom that will benefit you the rest of your life. Learn this and you will open the door to true love. In this section you will discover the secrets of the Don Juan, and we will also reveal the gullibility inside *you* that makes you fall prey to his charms.

Don't be surprised if you find something of yourself on these pages even if you have never rendezvoused with a "Don." I believe that most of us in this society, to one degree or another, suffer under the same illusions about love that the Don capitalizes on.

Warning: What you are about to read may change your life. It may completely destroy your illusions about love. I hope it does. Don't get me wrong; I believe in romance, I believe in true love, I believe in ideals of love. I even believe in the existence of soul mates. I certainly wouldn't want to tamper with any of that.

But I know that *illusions* distort and destroy love. They can make you feel so good, so complete . . . for the moment. But an illusion is garbage wrapped up in the finest wrapping. It is a gift from the devil himself. The end product is disappointment and disillusionment. (Did you get that word? dis*illusion*ment?) An illusion, by definition, is not real.

Did you ever meet someone who was always falling in love . . . and this time it was the real thing? This person probably had a time limit to his infatuations—a month, two months, or maybe even six months. And this person was probably very adept at blowing people off. Perhaps he was cruel about it, blaming his victim and indignantly pointing out her faults as if *he* were the injured party. Maybe he acted covertly and simply stopped calling, disappearing suddenly from his lover's life.

> "He was (my interpretation of) the ultimate in success, appearance, and sexuality; the playboy. Ours was a 'feather in the cap' affair, full of flattery and lies that led nowhere. Not only would he build me up, but dump me just as easily, yet his magnetism attracted me as long as I continued my self-destructive pattern."

These people can do a lot of damage to others. The character of Arnie Becker on "L.A. Law" is recognizable as a Don Juan, and so is that friend of yours who always has a new conquest. Let's take a look at Don Juan.

He idealizes love. He idealizes the woman he is currently pursuing. In a relationship, he is excited that he may have finally found the woman of his dreams. He is smitten by the woman he is involved with and powerless in her presence. But you would never think he feels powerless, because he exudes confidence. It is a false confidence; actually, it smacks of narcissism. In psychological terms, he never got past the narcissistic stage in his sexual development—which accounts for his boyish mannerisms and appeal. Women tend to like him for this boyishness because it makes him seem vulnerable. He is *not* vulnerable.

A Don Juan's persistence and devotion has roots in a deceit that even he can't see; he actually believes that what he has pretended is true. He is merely playing the role he thinks a man should play in a perfect love relationship. He plays it well and disappears as soon as you step out of the role he has selected for you.

The relationship is intense and volatile. If (when) he stops seeing you as perfect, it could be for any reason. He might be turned off when he notices a wart on your hand or a stain on your clothes, and it blows his whole image of you.

Usually he is a great lover. He fulfills your every desire. He has idealistic principles about sex and will be genuinely troubled if he can't make you come. Like a teenager, he has an attitude of invincibility about himself, and is irresponsible about birth control, thinking getting someone pregnant or getting a disease are things that can't happen to him.

A Don Juan is a chameleon and can be whatever he needs to be to get you. As soon as he has you conquered (has sex with you, makes you reach orgasm, makes you stop seeing others, or meets any other item on his agenda), he is off to the next conquest. Perhaps he thought you were "the one," but when he didn't "see God" when he had his first orgasm with you, he figured that he had made a mistake. "Let's move on to the next potential soul mate."

He is in a position to not need you. Typically, he has women friends he doesn't sleep with, with whom he has his long-term relationships. Thus, he has the power to cut off his feelings and to be coldly logical. But the Don is not usually an evil-intentioned person. Somewhere in the Don Juan's childhood, his emotional growth was stunted. At some point, he learned to shut off painful feelings and try to make the best of things. So now he both wants and fears intimacy to an obsessive degree. At a deep level, he is in pain himself. (But feeling sorry for him isn't going to help him one damn bit.)

THE PROBLEM EXTENDS BEYOND HIM

The Don and his current affair are egged on and approved of by society. In Western culture, we propagate—even sell—romance myths. Very few people in our culture go into a relationship unburdened by such illusions and delusions. (The greater the number of illusions, the more disappointing the relationship.) Our "best" books, movies, and songs feed the illusion of giving in to passion, romance, intrigue, and mystery. Even as children, we were read stories about knights in shining armor saving damsels, and princes and princesses living happily ever after. So, while the Don Juan is a snake (albeit a lovable one) who will recklessly ruin your love life, he may also put his life on the line for some idealistic purpose. If Don Juan did not have his illusions, he would have to face some of the pain and conflict in his life. If you try to destroy his illusions, he might fight to the death for them and claim that you are cynical and don't believe in true love or romance.

So the truth here is that the Don is a *love addict*. Don't be smug; many of Don Juan's conquests are love addicts themselves. In fact, almost all of us have illusions about love, even when we don't think we do. You want real love? Get rid of your illusions. There is no perfect mate. There are no princes or knights in shining armor. No one is going to save your derriere, and no one is going to make you whole . . . except you.

Real love doesn't always come from attractive people. Sometimes it comes from people with saddlebags on their hips and blemishes on their skin. Real love comes from babies who mess in their diapers and old people to whom you have to repeat everything four times.

If you want to ruin a relationship, try to make it perfect instead of better. Try to make it ideal instead of real. It's wonderful to have ideals and to strive to have the best relationship you can. But realize that no relationship can be perfect—only illusions are perfect. Apply perfection to mathematics, not to people. As humans, we can expect only to get better . . . not perfect. Some of us are so pompous about perfection that we expect even more from ourselves and others than God does. Now *that* is pomposity!

The capability to love is given by grace alone. You get it up front, with no obligations. You can experience it now. However, intimacy, trust, and other essential, meaningful parts of a relationship are cultivated over time.

SEX IS PART OF THE PROBLEM, TOO

Even sex is best when cultivated over time. For the Don Juan, the sex in a relationship starts off with a big bang and then becomes less and less exciting. But in reality, when sex is part of a meaningful relationship, it becomes better and better as people get to know each other. I don't mean better in a racy way; I mean better as far as the feeling of wholeness and intimacy is concerned.

Humans are the only animals I know (other than animals kept in captivity) that rush into sex. I grew up on a farm and watched the squirrels, chipmunks, and other animals court each other through play. They don't just meet each other and "have at it."

When people rush into having sex, it seems their attention becomes focused on it, and some important processes are bypassed. It seems that once a relationship is consummated by sex, the relationship changes. Premature sexual relations are usually just sex, not a consummation of the relationship. Maybe someday someone will figure it all out, but for right now perhaps the best reason not to have sex first is just that it works better that way.

The Don Juan who continues his ways gets kinkier and kinkier. Sex becomes even more of an obsession. He then starts believing that love itself is an illusion since he can never seem to find it. He is looking in frilly (but empty) packages.

There seems to be a natural law that guarantees an end to destructive behavior. There are plenty of warning signs along the way, but people who don't pay attention eventually do themselves in. The con man's tricks become obvious. The Hitler becomes paranoid and commits suicide. The Don Juan becomes impotent.

THE NATURE OF ILLUSIONS

When you carry around an illusion (the Hollywood version of romantic love, that perfect mate, always-incredible sex), it is impossible for you and your mate to live up to it. You are loving an illusion instead of a real person. If you and your partner have to be Superman and Superwoman, you will inevitably fail, and you may be so ashamed of that failure you will let no one console you for your human frailty.

It's hard to stand out there without an illusion. You may feel naked and vulnerable. Illusions mask painful feelings. To give up an illusion means to finally confront those feelings. Giving up an illusion means confronting uncertainty. An illusion gives you the false confidence of thinking you know how it all works. But guess what? You *don't* know how it all works because it works differently each and every time.

Some people also feel sad or angry when they give up an illusion. They feel sad because the illusion was so comforting and beautiful to look forward to; there is a kind of beautiful sadness about the loss. We get angry because we can't have what we dreamed of.

On the giving up of illusions, I say with the greatest compassion, "Just let them go!" Experience whatever emotions you uncover along the way, whether they be feelings of loss, abandonment, sadness, anger, or any other natural feeling. . . . Be with your feelings. . . . Feel the feelings. Your scars will heal instead of turning malignant.

Put your hope in something real, like yourself, a higher power, or the wonder of other people, warts and all. There are so many people with the same illusions that sometimes it can be difficult to identify what is real, and this is where the Don Juan makes his entrance. He finds out what your illusions are, dresses himself up to look like them, gets what he wants, and leaves you feeling used.

The Don Juan is the extreme, but any of us can fall prey to illusions. For example, your spouse never lives up to your expectations. You can always point out someone else who is "better" than your mate. We are, in fact, a two-marriage society. The first marriage is fraught with illusion and becomes our learning experience. The second marriage is usually more realistic.

The idealism, hope, and principles of an illusion make them hard to give up and cause many stubborn people (not just Don Juan) to die holding onto them. It is like holding onto a piece of manure as if there is a diamond inside. These people will tell you that if they can't have "true love" then they don't want anything. So that's what they get—nothing, emptiness—perhaps with a few short periods of an unrealistic high. Would you want to settle for that?

If someone gives you love, appreciate it. Love cannot be earned. (If you think love can be earned, that's just another illusion.) You can only create an atmosphere in which love grows. If you give a Don Juan your love and he abuses it, distorts it, or uses it, it doesn't make you a fool. In the long run, *he* is the fool. But having unrealistic illusions *does* make you a fool. I don't know why people blame love for their pain. It's never the love that hurts.

If the foregoing killed some of your illusions, I don't apologize. In fact, you owe me. Your illusions can only contribute to the eventual demise of your love life. Just feel the feelings that your illusions have been holding back. Join the human race; be real. Then go out and love someone instead of being obsessed with them. Love someone in spite of the normal, human fear of rejection and abandonment. Be willing to be a fool. Take risks.

What if all this sounds too painful and you want to keep your illusions? Too late! You have already read this, and you know too much. Your illusions are going to start to die now whether you believe it or not. It will be all right. I know; I've been through it.

"For even as love crowns you, so shall he crucify you.
Even as he is for your growth, so is he for your pruning."
Kahlil Gibran, *The Prophet*

IF YOU'RE ATTRACTED TO DON JUANS

If any guy seems too good to be true, he probably is. If you always find yourself involved with men who either can't be faithful or expect you to live up to some impossible ideal, you must learn to watch for telltale signs of Don Juanism and take care not to send out the wrong signals.

- Be cautious if a man is too forthcoming. Few people launch into lengthy discussions of their finances, emotional health, or plans for the future at a party or on the first date.
- Watch out for a man who asks you a lot of questions, especially when his responding comments are suspicious: "Oh, really? I love fifteenth-century feminist poetry too!"
- Don't be afraid to ask questions about a man's dating history. If his past is full of women who "just didn't understand" him or were "too immature," chances are you'll fare no better than his past girlfriends.
- We all love romance, but be suspicious of any extreme efforts at romance that occur before love has blossomed. If he's taking you to Hawaii on your fourth date, it is a sign of a man overly anxious to impress.
- Be wary of a man who focuses all his attention on you. For healthy people, relationships are *one part* of their lives—they still have friends, jobs, and hobbies.
- Be careful that you are not always putting "your best foot forward." You may be trying to be too perfect, too. Let him see a picture of you as a chubby six-year-old. Don't clean up the apartment every time he comes over. Go without makeup a few times. Then see how he treats you.
- Stay away from places Don Juans tend to congregate— bars, singles clubs, certain types of health clubs—you

know, pick-up joints. Why make it hard on yourself?

- Show a guy you're dating that sometimes you like to just hang out with him. Make sure you're not spending every moment in a candlelit room looking into each other's eyes.
- Tell anyone you're seeing *flat out* if you feel he's idealizing you. "That's nice of you to say, Don, but I am not prettier than Miss America. It's important to me that you love me for who I really am." Or try "Don, it's no fun for me to feel as if I can't be myself with you. If we were perfect, life would be so boring! I do want to be the best I can, but please don't expect me to act as if I'm happy all the time—I'm just not. I can use a hug when I'm down. If you don't want to be the one to give it to me, that's fine, but I'm not going to pretend I'm not hurting just to please you."
- Don't idealize him. Notice his good qualities and compliment him on them, but be sure you're also aware of his flaws. He has to have some. Don't dwell on them, but if you think he's trying to appear godlike, let him know he's trying too hard. "You don't have to impress me with your accomplishments, Don. I like you no matter what you've done."
- Stop seeing a guy if you think he's wrapped up in illusions. You can't live up to his ideals, and you're going to end up getting hurt if you try. Resist the temptation to think it's "better to have loved and lost than to never have loved at all." That quotation applies to real love, not illusions. Besides, it's not better to waste your time on someone if it means you might be *missing* time with someone you can share real love with.

IF YOU'RE ALREADY WITH A DON JUAN

If you're already with a Don Juan, all the tips above apply to you, but if you're in really deep, you might decide you could use some help getting out. There are many Sex and Love Addicts Anonymous (SLAA) groups that are doing great things for Don Juans and the people they leave in their wakes. If you are used to working things out yourself, go ask someone for help for a change. If you get turned down, experience that and then ask for help from someone else who may be more of a real friend. And try to get your Don Juan into a group.

In the late seventies I belonged to an encounter group that met once a month on a Saturday. It was a group mostly for professionals in the psychology field. There was a man there who seemed to have a charisma about him that would make women notice him. He was always surrounded by women. A handsome man, he was in his forties and had been married a few times.

The participants split into groups, and it turned out that I was in an all-male group with him. During the discussion, it came out that the other men were envious of him and admired him for his way with women. He told us that anyone could be like him. As he began his story he had a "Here's how to do it, guys" tone.

He told us that he had studied women from the time he was ten years old. He had made it his mission to bed down as many women as he could. It was all he thought about. He got to the point where he could look at a woman and be able to tell exactly what he would have to do to get her in bed. He said he had to actually be the kind of person she would most likely go to bed with. If the woman seemed to be unattainable, it would become his obsession to have her, and he would never give up until he was able to charm her. The bigger the challenge, the better. The ones who resisted him the most, and for the longest, he would marry.

We asked him what he meant by "becoming the man of her dreams." He told us he had to be a chameleon, and he started to tell us how he did that. Then this big strapping man began to cry. We looked at each other questioningly.

One man went over and asked him what he was feeling. He held his head in his hands and said, "I don't know who I am. I've lost myself." It came out that his father had been something of a Casanova, and his mother had taken out her anger about it on her son. All he had ever wanted was for his mother to like him. Later he had been so busy changing his identity to try to get women to like him that he had lost himself. He was holding onto a lot of shame. He didn't feel worthy of his mother's love, so he didn't feel worthy of any woman's love. Whenever he got it, he would manipulate it, use it, and destroy it.

SLAA and other groups help people find out what causes their unproductive behavior and learn new, effective ways of dealing with others. It sounds funny to say that sometimes we have to *learn* to love in a healthy way, but if love is bringing us more pain than pleasure, we have no choice. We have to reassess our own lovableness as well as our ability to love. We also have to learn *whom* to love.

When I counsel single women, I notice a recurring theme: a woman will tell me that the guys she meets who would make good husbands and fathers don't turn her on; she always falls in love with the jerks. Let me tell you, the world is not filled with sexually unappealing nice guys and sexy jerks. If you view the world this way, the problem is not out there, in the world, but *in there*, inside you. There are plenty of women married to good husbands with whom they are totally in love, and the sooner you resolve the internal conflict that is making you overromanticize love, the sooner the right man will walk into your life.

THE LIAR

We all have come into contact with a Liar. The guy you're dating says he'll marry you as soon as he gets his promotion, but when he gets it, he gives you another reason why you must wait. Your lover swears to be true, yet you find him with someone else. Your husband snickers at the outfit your friend is wearing at a party, but then he gushes over her, telling her how nice she looks. The "rich" man you meet at a bar has expensive clothes and drives an expensive car; later you find out he's $50,000 in debt.

Once you find out the guy you love is a Liar, the fun stops. You can't count on him, don't know when to believe him, and end up wondering if there's any depth to him at all. But, like the Don Juan, the Liar is extremely seductive. The web he weaves, even if it is woven with lies, can be very enticing. When he tells you you're beautiful, it's wonderful to hear (until you find out he doesn't really think so at all). When he says "I'll take you away from all this," it's tempting to think that he can and will.

Some liars are terrible at lying. They're easy to spot and it is not a real hardship to stay away from them. The ones to watch out for are the ones who are smooth and subtle. Some of these men lie for what they think is the good of others. If confronted, they respond with "I didn't want to hurt your feelings," or "I just thought it would make you happy." Others lie out of self-interest. Some are so caught up in their lies that they actually believe they're true (more on that later).

It is important to note that there is little difference between unconscious and conscious lying. If I drive through a mud puddle and splash you with water, it doesn't matter if I meant to or not, or if I even knew I had done it. You end up wet and dirty. Remember this about lies: A lie is a lie, period. Whatever the reason behind it, it distorts reality.

I'm not making any value judgments about lying here. We *all* lie sometimes. There are books and books on the ethics of lying, if you are interested in delving into moral issues. There are people who believe that "social" lying has its merit. They may be right. It may make sense to lie when you're trying not to hurt someone's feelings. What I'm talking about here is a practical issue. Look at it this way: if someone lies to you on a regular basis or about big things, it's not doing either of you any good.

> "My first husband practiced his skills throughout a fifteen-year relationship that ended in divorce, draining me of self-esteem and any love for him or myself. His specialties were lying, covering up, reversing the blame, the silent treatment, temper tantrums, and degrading me in front of a group."

Let's say your boyfriend spends a good five minutes at dinner one night telling you how beautiful he thinks you are. He talks about your hair, your eyes, your toenails. A few days later, at a party, you overhear him telling a friend that, while he doesn't think you're that good-looking, you're really sweet and smart and he thinks you're great. Now imagine how you feel. The love of your life has just said that you're sweet and smart (qualities that you probably admire more in people than good looks), yet you know he's lied to you. Blatantly! He thinks you're ugly, or at least not too attractive. If he'd never mentioned your looks to you at all, but simply told you the truth—that he thinks you're smart and sweet—you would have been very happy. But his compulsion to lie has left you feeling angry and confused. (Let's not even get into his discussing you so clinically with his friend!)

The bottom line is this: Life and having relationships are hard enough without adding falsehoods to the mix. As I described in the chapter on misunderstanding, sometimes communication between the sexes is difficult even under the best of circumstances.

LYING AS A WAY OF LIFE

If your partner makes a habit of lying to you, he may actually believe his own lies. I know that sounds hard to believe, but let me explain: Lying successfully brings the feeling of really having pulled something off (think about times you've gotten away with it yourself). If you can put your guilt aside, getting away with lying feels terrific. It is like getting something you really wanted for a fraction of the going price, but better. You control the outcome, and you are able to use your creativity and imagination in making it happen. It seems as if there is no price to pay for it and nobody gets hurt. Well, the relationship gets hurt, because trust is eroded, and the Liar himself is hurt as well. Nobody gets something for nothing in this world. There is always a price.

Think about it: if you are at a casino, and they know that it is your first time gambling at a casino, they will go out of their way to make sure you win. Why? So you get hooked. A drug dealer will give you expensive drugs for free—the first time. Why? So you get hooked. Perhaps you understand that but can't see how lying is exactly the same. Well, the first time your man lies to you successfully, he might get away with it. He begins to get hooked. It may not be a big deal to him because he thinks he has total control over his lying. He can stop anytime he wants to. But, like drugs or getting something for nothing (like gambling), lying changes a person's reality.

OK, so what's wrong with distorting reality a little? Well, when a person who does drugs begins to hallucinate, not only is he "in a different world," but his ability to operate in the real world is hampered. Think of people you've seen high or drunk. In that condition, they wouldn't function well in an office setting, in a car, or even writing a letter, although they may believe they are functioning well. In the same way, a gambler begins to see everything as one big game. If he's very far gone, he'll bet on anything—that the roach on his counter will turn left, that he can cross a busy highway in ten seconds. You can imagine how effective he is in daily life.

Lying puts a man in a different reality, too. If he lies and gets results, it's easier the next time, and the next time. Pretty soon it's easier to lie than to tell the truth. It is after he gets really good at it that he begins to believe his own lies. Because he designs it, the reality he creates when he lies is preferable to him than the reality the world lives in. He loses touch with people, creating his own private world. After that, little by little, he becomes more and more obvious. At some point he loses himself.

Within a Liar is someone who is not satisfied with who he is. He feels inadequate and unchangeable. Perhaps someone made him feel he was not good enough; he figures he can at least change the way he is perceived. And by lying, he is able to not only change the way others see him, but also to change the way he perceives himself. After a while, lying becomes a crutch he will use until he finds his real self-worth; yet he will never find his real self-worth when he is lying. His lying and his repression of the fact that he is doing so warp his mind. More lying calls for more repression, which warps the mind more. It is a one-way trip.

Lying feeds a person's egotism but not his self-esteem. If a man presents himself as different from what he really is and others admire him, he knows somewhere deep down that people are not admiring the *real* him. It's hard to be in a relationship with a man whose self-esteem is this fragile. His diminished sense of self coupled with the condescension he can feel for the people who believe his lies often lead him into other nasty-man behavior—in fact, a Liar can very easily become like any of the other types of nasty men outlined in this book, from the Cro-Magnon Man to the Physical Batterer.

HOW CAN YOU TELL SOMEONE IS LYING?

Some experts say when someone is lying he exhibits some of the following physical behaviors.

- He looks at you sideways instead of straight on, or he doesn't look at you at all.
- He twiddles his hand or finger.
- He strokes his hair or beard.
- He looks at you directly with a blank (innocent?) look. Actually, he is not really looking at *you*. He is, in his head, trying to think of what to say next.
- He taps his foot or shakes his leg.
- He alternates the blank look with not looking at you.

Of course his exhibition of any of this physical behavior is not *proof* that he is lying. He could be nervous or self-conscious because he is a nonconfrontational person. Or he could be someone who was made to feel guilty all his life. But it could be that he is nonconfrontational, guilt-ridden . . . and lying.

There are also expert Liars who show no physical signs of lying. An expert Liar, however, might show some of the following subtle psychological signs.

- He is perfectly confident in what he is saying because he knows he is lying.
- He is able to rationalize every single detail.
- He acts angry or hurt if you question him.
- He attacks you to get the attention off himself.
- He causes you to introvert (tries to get you to cave in), accusing you of being insecure, having a devious mind, or not trusting him. He is, of course, projecting his own problems onto you.

Rationalization is another tipoff to lying. When a person is rationalizing, he is usually in his own internal world (figuring everything out) and will tend to rationalize everything while in this mode. He probably can't stop. The conversation that follows is an example of this.

You: I saw your car parked in front of Jack's Sports Bar last night.
He: There are a lot of cars that look like mine.
You: Yes, but this one had your initials in the door.
He: Oh, I forgot! Bill borrowed my car last night.
You: OK. Hey! What do you think about Stephanie's new computer?
He: Well, it sure was expensive, but her parents have money, so what the heck. If you have it, why not use it?

Bingo! His third answer was a rationalization where there was clearly no need to rationalize. He was in "rationalization mode," and is probably lying. He was probably at the bar. Check it out.

When He Is Telling the Truth

- He may say, with apparent sincerity, something like, "I can't make you believe me."
- He probably won't get defensive, since he knows he has not been deceptive.
- He will probably make a sincere effort to identify any possible misunderstanding.
- His attitude may reflect that it is not his problem if you don't believe him.
- He may exhibit a quiet confidence without rationalizing, putting you down, getting defensive, or getting upset.

Of course, these are only clues. If you are constantly

accusing him of lying and you have not caught him in a lie, then it is perfectly normal for him to get annoyed with you after a time. If this is the case, then maybe you should stop accusing him and wait until you actually have something concrete. You may want to look at your mistrust and see if it is justified. Perhaps someone lied to you in the past, and you are taking it out on him. Or, if you are a Liar yourself, you could be projecting.

WHAT YOU CAN DO

There are a few things you can try if your man is lying to you. He'd do best with some professional psychological help, but chances are he's not exactly going to jump at the suggestion—he's not in the reality that sees lying as a problem.

Help Him Feel Lovable

Since a man lies to change a reality he is not happy with, it can help to show him that he doesn't need to lie. Praise his good qualities. Cuddle him. Help him feel safe just being himself. In the same way, accept with enthusiasm any of his efforts at making *you* feel lovable.

Let Him Know You Know

The old saying "Deep down, he wants to be caught" is true. He'll feel a sense of relief knowing that the truth is out. Don't listen to his protestations of innocence. If someone lies to you and then he admits it, *you* certainly feel better than if he denies it and tells you more lies to convince you; he probably does, too. Do not shame him (he has probably had enough of that already, from himself). Don't let him talk about how trust is a part of love, and don't listen when he says that if you love him, you should trust him. Love has nothing to do with trust. You certainly don't love him *be-*

cause you trust him. If that were the case, there would be no basis for the love. No, you love him because you love him. But, because he lies, you don't trust him. Trust is earned, not given and not deserved. Trust is certainly an important part of any relationship (think how you would feel if you found out a friend was taking $20 out of your wallet every now and then), but it is more of a practical issue than an emotional issue.

Make Sure There Are Consequences

Make him accountable for his lies. Do it lovingly, but be tough about it. Simply refuse to tolerate the lying. Speak in terms of how you feel about being deceived instead of attacking his self-esteem. This is *his* problem, and you do not want to be affected by it. Tell him that if you are affected, there will be consequences. If you don't think you are capable of approaching your man in this manner, see the discussion on confronting him in Chapter 7.

Here is how one woman confronted her husband about lying.

She: I want to talk with you about something very serious.

He: What?

She: Last Friday, you told me that you had to work overtime, and you got home after midnight with beer on your breath.

He: Well, I was working with some of the guys, and we stopped for a beer after.

She: I know what you did. You left work about eight o'clock and went to that go-go dancer club off the freeway.

He: (sheepishly) I know how you feel about those places, and I didn't want to hurt your feelings. All the guys went and I didn't want to be the only one who didn't go. It was a retirement party for Al, and I've been friends with him for a long time.

She: (angrily) I just want you to know that lying to me is a very serious matter and is ten times worse than going to that club. If I can't believe you, I can't trust you. Nothing you say to me will matter, and our relationship will deteriorate beyond repair. I have to know that you will not lie to me. If I can't know that, then I can't have a relationship with you. If you think this is no big thing, let me know now, because either you will have to leave or I will leave. It *is* a big thing, you see.

　　If you had told me you were going to that place, I *would* have been angry! I have a right to my feelings. But you have no right to lie to me. You have no right to try to manipulate my feelings. How many other times have you lied to me? I feel like a fool.

He: I'm sorry. It won't happen again.

She: You are going to have to convince me it won't happen again. I want to know what you are going to do about it. I'm not punishing you. I *really* need to know what you are going to do about it.

　　He couldn't come up with any suggestions, except to say he wouldn't lie anymore. She told him that was not good enough. She told him she didn't trust him the same as she had before, and she couldn't stand always wondering whether he was lying or not. He asked her for a suggestion. She said that she wanted him to sit down and think of all the times he had lied to her and write them down, including the times he twisted the truth and the times he had deceived her by *not* telling her things.

　　He did that, and she told him that would wipe the slate clean for now but also told him not to be surprised if she checked out some of his stories in the future until she felt comfortable with him again. She also told him that since he had lied to her, she could never completely trust him again and that there might be times when she would doubt him. And when she did doubt him, she would be checking out his story and confronting him with any deception.

Since the husband really did want to stop lying and he loved and trusted his wife, he allowed her to be "the enforcer" in his efforts to stop lying. In every other aspect their marriage remained the same—they were equals—but regarding this issue he let her be the "boss" for a while. He made a real effort to stop lying (to her *and* to himself), and she confronted him every time she caught him backsliding. He was very, very careful about telling her the truth, and made an effort to be honest with himself as well. Before long, he got used to telling the truth, and it became second nature where lying had been before. He was greatly relieved not to have to worry about being caught all the time; he hadn't realized how much of a strain it had been to be a Liar. She began to trust him again.

If your guy just hasn't grown up in this aspect of his life, perhaps you can help him. But then again, he may be an incurable, pathological liar. You will have to make a decision about how harmful his lies are and how far gone he is. Once you have determined this, you must decide what you are going to do about your relationship with him.

THE CRO-MAGNON MAN

A Cro-Magnon Man is one who isn't very "evolved." He likes to do his own thing so much that he doesn't even notice that other people have needs. Though coworkers and neighbors may think the world of him, people who really know him think he defines the word "selfish." He has an uncanny ability to get what he wants by simply taking it, even if it hurts someone else. And although he cares a lot about what other people think of him, he is prone to taking advantage of those whom he knows love him or look up to him. He invalidates others by using them, ignoring them, or avoiding them.

Cro-Magnon Man is just not very deep. He has no concept of what you mean when you say you'd like more intimacy. He has trouble connecting with others; many of his "important" relationships are superficial ones. On close examination, he appears to be lacking in higher consciousness. This is not to say the Cro-Magnon Man may not be a religious person. But as a religious person he would most likely be ritualistic and believe in rules literally, rather than understand the intent of his religion, the big picture, or the overall purpose of it. He is capable of understanding the superficialities of life and may be very adept at dealing with them when it comes to survival or comfort issues, but it is very unlikely that you would ever see him reading a book like this one. It's not that he is unintelligent, but it seems he often lacks compassion and understanding. A conversation with him just does not *feel* very fulfilling.

There are two types of Cro-Magnon Men: one exhibits some of the behavior of a Cro-Magnon but is not one in his heart of hearts; the other is the incurable Cro-Magnon, who probably doesn't even *have* a heart of hearts. Both types want to be perceived as good and, to avoid emotion, are careful not to do anything really wrong, and are masters of omission. For the sake of clarification, let's call the first one "Mr. Niceguy" and the other one "Mr. Skindeep."

MR. NICEGUY

Oops! There he is, walking on the clean carpet in his muddy boots, and he left the door open again. So you shut the door and get out the spot cleaner one more time. Did he remember to pick up some bread on the way home from work? Nooo! And he seems as distressed about it as you are. He seems to be his own worst enemy. You have become familiar with his routine over the last several years. Are you really . . . angry? No, you're livid . . . No, the word is *pissed*. You feel like screaming, yet there is that part of you that feels sorry for him, because you can see that he doesn't want to be this way but can't seem to help it.

You settle down, and things get back to normal. But normal means he's still taking his time getting ready when you go out—you're always late because of him and it's getting irritating. Or he falls asleep on the couch even though you had a "date" to make love. He leaves dishes soaking in the sink, even though it was his turn to do them, but he manages to get the car waxed (something he enjoys doing) and the paper read. You agree that little Johnny shouldn't have ice cream for breakfast, but there's Johnny grinning from ear to ear, his mouth gooey with chocolate mint crunch.

Sometimes you get so frustrated with your partner that you want to vent your anger at him by invalidating him, and then you feel bad—either for thinking it or for doing it—because he does have a good heart, and he is so nice to you. He can be so affectionate and patient. You just can't get over what a bitch you are at times, and you think, "Well, I have my problems, too." But it seems that no one can bring out the bitch in you better than he can. You go through all your faults in your mind and try to think of what you might be doing to cause this turmoil. Certainly, you can't blame it all on him(?).

If he wasn't such a nice guy, some of the things he does would seem rude. But he is just so oblivious that you know he doesn't do these things purposely. Some of the things he does make him seem so uncaring, yet you know he cares. Still, you're tired of feeling disappointed in him, and in your relationship.

Your life with him is miserable, yet you can't think of any major crime he has committed against you, just misdemeanors—a *whole lot* of misdemeanors. Sometimes you wish he *would* do something deliberate. Anything! That's one of his major problems: He is not deliberate. He doesn't *mean* to forget to pick you up and he didn't *mean* those words that hurt you. There is always an excuse or lie and a lack of purposefulness.

People have "had a talk with him," yelled at him out of frustration, and invalidated him. He takes it in his stride and never seems to hold a grudge against them. He just accepts it as a part of his life, and he even agrees with their complaints about him. He is sometimes frustrated by his own ways, but has given up on himself and doesn't know how to change.

Feelings? What Feelings?

When you do something that would normally upset someone, Mr. Niceguy acts as if it doesn't bother him . . . but then he may forget your anniversary. Even though it may look as if he is deliberately forgetting, that is usually not so.

It is just that he is so out of touch with certain feelings that he doesn't even know he has them. And because he is out of touch with certain feelings, he doesn't recognize them in others either. He can't imagine why you are so upset that he tracked mud on the carpets, because if *you* had done that, it wouldn't really bother him. He thinks he is simply surrounded by people who get upset easily and who are too rigid about life. He looks down on people in a way, because he believes their emotions are out of control. However, he sees that they are really bothered by these "insignificant" things, so he tries to be nice about it. He plays along with them, thinking he is being kind by not insulting them or making light of things they think are important. Besides, he doesn't want to get into a confrontation with them. He will agree to whatever they want, and then do as he pleases.

The fashionable term for this kind of behavior is *passive-aggressive*. But when people use this label, they often shade it with blame, which I do not like. Somewhere, in his childhood possibly, this guy probably learned to deal with painful emotions by blocking them out. Perhaps grave consequences resulted from showing his anger. In any case, he is so far away from his feelings that he doesn't acknowledge them at all. He appears to let things roll off his back (something he wishes you would do more often). He avoids conflict at all cost. It is easier to "forget" than to deal with his feelings. He may even lie to you to avoid a confrontation with emotions (yours or his). The bottom line is that when Mr. Niceguy starts to feel anger, he deals with it by squelching it. But the anger does not just go away. The repression of the anger merely turns the problem over to the unconscious. It may manifest in ulcers, forgetfulness, resistance to sexual advances, or being too tired to go out to dinner.

Rather than blame the guy or label him, it is more useful to look at where he is coming from. If he can't deal with his own feelings, you can't expect him to deal with yours. He is afraid of your feelings, because if he acknowledges your feelings, he may have to acknowledge his own, and he just doesn't know how. Punishing him, nagging him, or invalidating him are not going to help. He will just try harder to become nicer, which will fuel his unconscious with anger and result in more of the forgetfulness, airheadedness, or distancing.

If you do push him further, he may actually try to turn the tables on you, suggesting that *you* are the one who has all this hostility, and since everyone else thinks he is a great guy, it must be *you* who has the problem (but hey, they don't live with him). He may finally tell you all the things that bother him about *you*. This may be a healthy catharsis for him, but he will resent you for pushing him into a state of conflict. To him, happiness is a plane of existence on which there is no conflict. He may have had so much conflict early in his life and have so many buried feelings that he just can't take any more. He is "happy" and relieved on that plane of no conflict, not realizing that he can live on other, higher planes of existence once he is able to get in touch with his feelings and unload his pent-up past.

Being nice to him won't help either. All that does is let him continue his "blissful" existence (he's not really happy, just relieved). He will continue to skirt his responsibilities, possibly to the point that you become his "mom," and continue in his narcissistic selfish ways. Every so often, he may apologize for his behavior, try to make it up to you, or acknowledge that you do more than your fair share. These are glimmers of consciousness, not revelations leading to real change.

MR. SKINDEEP

Mr. Skindeep is a different type of Cro-Magnon altogether. He may act like Mr. Niceguy, but he is different. He may be the same in the way he avoids conflict, but he avoids it because he doesn't really give a damn. Mr. Skindeep is not unconsciously passive-aggressive; "deliberately vengeful" is more descriptive. If he forgets things, it is usually because from the first he had no intentions of doing what you asked.

He doesn't have the heart of Mr. Niceguy, and he is not really well meaning.

Mr. Skindeep is very good at copying behavior (like any intelligent monkey), but he is not really capable of higher thought, ethics, or spirituality. He can be very fun-loving, handsome, earthy—he can emulate any kind of behavior you may like to see in a man. He can also pretend he is a deeper person than he really is, perhaps by being quiet and mysterious about his views on higher matters, but he probably could not sustain the pretense for very long without exposing himself.

He may appear to be confident. It is just arrogance. He may appear to be decisive. He just knows what he wants. Perception is more important to him than truth. All he cares about is how he is perceived.

If Mr. Skindeep does something for you, he feels you owe him (for example, sex for dinner). He is incapable of spending time with a woman just to be with her. He always has an ulterior motive (sex, control, curiosity).

This guy demands dedication, loyalty, and dinner at five with the minimum hassle. He picks the friends and relatives you are allowed to spend your time with—and that would be as little time as possible. You depend on him financially, and he has worn you down to an emotional cripple, making you dependent on him for any bones he may throw your way. He thinks love is a weakness women have that enables men to dominate them.

Mr. Skindeep doesn't mean to hurt you, but he's like a crocodile. The crocodile floats in the water with a big smile on his face. If he is not hungry, he won't eat you. If he is hungry he will snap you up and roll you over before you know what hit you. Crocodiles eat their young if food is in short supply. This man may really care about you (as much as he is capable of caring), but he cares more about what he wants. If you supply what he wants, he may give you what he thinks you want. If you do not, he'll say, "Aw, hon. You understand, don't you? Life is about me, me, me."

"He was good at making me feel I was going crazy—right down to the suggestion I see a psychiatrist because he cared for me and wanted me to get better. Ironically, the person who gave me *Nasty People* was my mother-in-law. She brought it over to my house under her coat. She did not want my father-in-law to know she had the book or had read it. That tells us who the original invalidator was. She has become a severe alcoholic. I refuse to live my life that way."

Don't Bother Looking Deeper: There's Nothing There

Don't expect Mr. Skindeep to be stupid, poor, or obvious. The logic section of his brain may be just as developed as anyone else's. He can be very clever, very funny, or very rich, but he will always be superficial. I have never seen a true Mr. Skindeep develop into a spiritual, sensitive human being. I'd like to see it happen, but never have. Mr. Skindeep asks himself only two questions: What is best for me? and What can I get away with and still come out looking like a decent guy?

For Mr. Skindeep, a wife and a family are things to be reckoned with, rather than things for which he provides comfort and support. Dedication and loyalty seem like foolish qualities to him, good only in that they can be used to manipulate others.

One way to understand Mr. Skindeep is to think about biology. A cell is an entity on its own, but it cannot survive long by itself. The cell *is* the organism, as are the other cells, and as the organism *is* the cells. There is a part of a person that *is* family and *is* society. When a cell does its own thing, it's called cancer.

A person exists as an individual (individual-self); as part of many personal relationships (relationship-self); as part of a group such as a business, church, family, or community (group-self); and as part of mankind (mankind-self). His total self is actually a composite of all of these.

We all have these component "selves," and each is developed to a greater or lesser degree in each of us. They require a balance. If a person has an illness that is contagious, it may be better for her group-self if she stays home from work rather than infect others. If a woman has been stuck home all week with the kids, it may be better if her husband takes her out on a date rather than watching football. One man will throw himself on a grenade to save his fellow soldiers. Another individual (like Mother Teresa) might make the betterment of mankind her life's work. The daily balance of the aspects of each of the selves is what is most important.

A Mr. Skindeep needs to better develop his relationship-self. The cure for selfishness lies in the development of the group-self. Because in a way, a man is there to serve his family, to help them and to see that they are treated fairly. He can do this more effectively if he knows he *is* his family. He represents the male world, *is* the male world to his children. He may be an electrician or a lawyer, a fun-loving guy or reserved one, but there is one thing he *must* do. He must be able to *be* his family. He must be able to ask, "What is good for my family? What is good for me?" He must be able to give each of those questions the proper weight. He must not be a person who thinks only about what is good for his individual-self.

A true Mr. Skindeep *will* not (as opposed to *can* not) transform into a family-oriented man. If he stands to lose everything he may *act* transformed, but as soon as he has nothing to lose, his basic self-centeredness will reappear.

IS YOUR MAN HOPELESSLY SUPERFICIAL?

The chart below is meant to help you gauge or give you a general feel for the type of Cro-Magnon you are dealing with.

Developed Man	**Mr. Niceguy**	**Mr. Skindeep**
Confident	Egotistical	Arrogant
Centered	Preoccupied	Self-centered
Ethics come before his wants and needs	His ethics are rationalized	His wants and needs come before ethics
Directly confronts when necessary	Avoids confrontation	Invalidates, attacks
Knows his perspective is only *his* perspective	Wants to know what *your* perspective is so he can fit in with it	Thinks his perspective of life is the way it is
Likes to be right	Lets you be right all the time	Needs to appear right
Loves you	Loves you and wants to please you into loving him	Expects you to love him
Has self-esteem	Mixed egotism and self-esteem	Egotism
Evaluates	Looks for an "out"	Judges, generalizes
Kind	Acts kind so you'll think he's kind	Mistakes kindness as weakness or as a favor he owes
Enjoys doing favors for others	Feels he *has* to do favors for others	Does things for you so you'll owe him
Capable of mutual give and take	Overt giver, covert taker	A taker

Developed men are not perfect, and they will exhibit Cro-Magnon behavior at times. You will definitely see a Cro-Magnon man exhibiting the behavior of a developed man at times, but he is just mimicking. Most men do go through a Cro-Magnon stage sometime during their adolescence. For the Cro-Magnon, that is the peak of his development.

IF YOU'RE INVOLVED WITH A MR. SKINDEEP

If you are currently involved with a Mr. Skindeep, you know it deep down. The man isn't just hiding from his soul; his soul is asleep. And he has no intention of waking up—it might "weaken" him.

There are many women who have had vast experience trying to change a Mr. Skindeep, and they will tell you that they wasted their effort, time, even their lives. They thought he would change after a significant life event like marriage or having a child. All these women ever got was more of the same. Trying to change Mr. Skindeep will absolutely guarantee your failure.

You might not like hearing this because you love this man, are attached to him, obsessed with him, dependent on him, and so on. You may think I am giving you no hope. As long as you think you can change him, or that he will want to change himself, I can give you no hope. You may be one of those "never say die" people who won't quit because you don't want to admit failure. If you get stuck in an unrealistic hope, it will stop you from moving on to more practical ways of dealing with things. The sooner you give up hope of ever changing this man, the sooner you can move on to a more meaningful and enjoyable life. Why put up with misery?

It might help to remember that Mr. Skindeep is human only in the most general sense of the word. I am reminded of a little story that seems to fit this situation. There once was a caring, nurturing woman, who found a snake half-dead near a stream. The woman took the snake home, nursed its wounds, fed it, and loved it. The snake began to get well, but surely would have died if the woman had not taken care of it. One day the woman went to check on the snake, and the snake bit her with its poisoned fangs. As the woman lay on the floor dying, she said to the snake, "I don't understand. I saved your life, and now you have killed me." The snake said, "Well, you knew I was a snake when you found me, didn't you?!"

HOW TO HANDLE MR. NICEGUY

Some women have a very difficult time standing up to Mr. Niceguy. After all, he looks like a total prince to everyone else. If you're with one yourself, you may have complained about him only to hear "But he's so funny!" or "But he seems to love you so much!" or "You just don't know how lucky you are." Well, you're not lucky. Don't ignore the way you *feel*. No one else lives with this guy (except maybe his kids, and they're another reason he ought to get his act together).

The first and most important thing you can do for yourself when you're with a Mr. Niceguy is to take *your relationship* to counseling. What I mean is, ask him to go for the sake of your relationship. It may take a little kicking butt, but he's afraid of losing you so he'll probably go. Perhaps (I hope) the counselor will recommend some sort of group therapy for him so he can get feedback about the way he affects others and get in touch with his feelings. That will be nice for him, but what about you? There was probably a reason you were attracted to him, and there is probably something you find appealing in this kind of relationship. Try to focus on yourself and your relationship, not on him. As I said, take the *relationship* to counseling.

There are also two things you can do to help create a growth environment for Mr. Niceguy. The first is to create an atmosphere that is loving, warm, and accepting . . . maybe the opposite of what he grew up with. This may take incredible patience and focus from you; you won't be able to simultaneously point out his faults and be accepting of his emotions, which would give him mixed signals. You would have to accept all his emotions as just emotions and reward the smallest show of them.

He needs to switch from taking blame to taking responsibility for his actions (avoiding his old avoidances, taking ownership of his acts of omission). You can encourage the further development of your Mr. Niceguy by refusing—in a friendly, humorous way—to take on the role of his mother. Stop shielding him from the consequences of his behavior. Take the dishes he left undone overnight and put them under his pillow. Take the dirty socks and underwear he left on the floor and put them in his toolbox, and let them accumulate there. If he is overweight, tell him (in a nice way) that since you want him to live longer, you will not purchase soda and ice cream for him. Let him run out of deodorant if he forgets to put it on the shopping list. If he is more than fifteen minutes late, leave without him. Don't *reason* with him, just communicate nonverbally in terms of consequences.

Because Mr. Niceguy usually doesn't have an overt problem such as alcoholism or violent behavior, it may seem tempting to ignore your situation. Many wives do just that and live out unfulfilling lives married to guys who look great on the outside but give them no emotional fulfillment and often no fun. Therapy, especially marital therapy, is a proven method of dealing with what is really *the guy's* problem. (It is also her problem because she's with him. Even if she were capable of having a fulfilling relationship with another man, it doesn't matter because she is not with another man; she's with *this* man.) But if you're going to stay with Mr. Niceguy, you should realize, in the interest of keeping yourself emotionally healthy, that *you are not his therapist*. Even if you were a renowned psychologist, you wouldn't be able to help him. (Ask any renowned psychologist with a spouse and family!) You can't reparent him, primal-scream him, or psychoanalyze him. It's not appropriate for your relationship; it cannot work. But you can change your relationship with him to break the destructive cycles you may be stuck in. You may be surprised, once a cycle is broken, how receptive your man is to growth.

If your Mr. Niceguy is feeling especially threatened because you have been on him for not helping you out around the house or not sharing his feelings with you, he may have reached the point where he's lashing out at you fairly regularly (in private, of course). Some of the tips in the Verbal Batterer chapter may be of help in breaking that pattern and getting back to the point where you can rationally discuss going to a marriage counselor or changing some of the ground rules of the relationship (that is, letting him know the consequences of his behavior).

One more thing: Almost *every* man has some of the traits of Mr. Niceguy. It is a matter of degree. Take inventory of your traits. Are you a perfectionist? Do you have realistic expectations of the human man you love, or do you really want a superhuman being who will anticipate your every need and fit your image of what a man *should* be? If so, then I think it would be healthy and less frustrating for you to adopt a different attitude. If you can't get what you want, it may be important to *want what you have*.

THE PHYSICAL BATTERER

If you are with a man who strikes you, pushes you, beats you, or is in any way physically violent toward you, run, don't walk, away from him—as soon as you can. He doesn't need you; he needs professional help. Your children, however, if you have any, *do* need you, and you're doing them no favor by risking your life or letting them see this kind of behavior. I know it's hard to leave someone you love or once loved. The last chapter of this book, "Stand Up," may inspire you to take the big step, but maybe you'd be better off calling a local battered women's shelter—or the local police—*now*.

Do you think your situation is different and your man is special? He may have some terrific qualities, but the two of you are locked in a terrible cycle and he is not going to be the one to break it. You have to.

Many women (and I hope *most* women) would never put up with a physical beating. It is such an obvious and extreme form of invalidation that they refuse to put up with it. No matter how much they loved their men, and no matter how otherwise charming and wonderful the men were, one incident would be enough, and they would be out the door. The subject of battering has been in the news and in movies recently. It is of great interest because of the absurdity of the phenomenon; it just doesn't fit with what most people believe can happen. It is an extreme example of what can indeed happen when people get stuck in a bad mind-set.

WHY IT HAPPENS

More often than not, the physically battered woman who stays in the relationship shares her batterer's perceptions. What follows may get your dander up, so be prepared. Here it is: In their perception, the needs, wishes, and priorities of the man are more important than those of the woman. When the man hits the woman, it is because she did something to cause it. There are circumstances under which it is OK for the man to beat the woman. Sometimes she deserves a beating.

Some of the men and women who subscribe to this reality are what we consider well educated. They can be ministers, doctors, and other professionals. But educated or not, most of these men come from abusive backgrounds.

The Physical Batterer has a fear of being deserted or abandoned, so he tries to control all situations through dominance, fear, or threats. He is very manipulative in his primary relationship and will do whatever he feels he has to do to keep it in line. He has the ability to distort reality and make it sound convincing, often playing on his partner's morality or compassion. He blames her for getting him upset. He is also overly jealous. If a male stranger says hello to a Physical Batterer's partner, the abuser may tell her that her skirt is too short and she looks like a whore. He may accuse her of having an affair with the stranger. His insecurities are insurmountable, and his dependency on her is so great that he feels he will die psychologically if she leaves. Because of his intense need to control and manipulate her, he eventually causes the very thing he fears most, and she leaves him.

It is true that a woman can be very abusive to a man, emotionally and verbally. Still this is *never* justification for a man to hit her. If the roles were reversed and she was physically abusive to him, I would have the same advice for him: leave! Physical abusers need counseling, and 95 percent of the time they have to be forced into getting it.

The physically battered woman is usually from a home that had an absentee or emotionally distant father. Her knowledge of men in general (other than abusive men) is minimal; she lacks any real knowledge of how other men behave. With no realistic concept of how normal male-female relationships work, she wants nothing more than to be noticed—and approved of—by men, so she becomes the ultimate pleaser, ready and willing to be imposed upon. She is generally very reliable. She also has a tendency to believe what a man says. She believes him when he tells her that he would not have beaten her if she hadn't burned the spaghetti sauce. She tries to control him by pleasing him, and she thinks that if she just doesn't burn the spaghetti sauce, everything will be all right.

The abuser and victim typically go through a cycle: there is a period of stress, followed by an explosion, followed by a honeymoon period.

HOW IT HAPPENS

Stress

During the stress period, the Physical Abuser begins to have fears. He thinks his partner is getting too independent, he is afraid she will leave him, or he feels he just needs to establish his power and control. To keep her one down and off balance, he will scrutinize everything she does, question her every move. Nothing pleases him. He may use any of the techniques that the Verbal Batterer uses. (Most women say that the psychological abuse is worse than the physical abuse.) The uncertainty, the feeling of having to walk on eggshells, is very trying for the woman during this tension-building stage. Sometimes the woman even provokes the physical abuse so she can just get it over with and move on to the "honeymoon" period. This may cause some foolhardy people to believe that she actually wants the beating.

> "He spent a lot of time trying to [verbally] invalidate me. I guess it didn't work because finally he became physically violent."

Explosion

The Physical Batterer finally finds something he can use as an excuse for his rage, and he takes it out on the woman physically. These explosions are often accompanied ("caused") by the use of alcohol or other drugs that loosen inhibitions. After he has released all his anger and rage, he is usually very remorseful. He will be very sorry and blame his behavior on the liquor or on some specific thing she did and make it sound very convincing (to her—it probably would not sound very convincing to you and me).

Honeymoon

During the "honeymoon," which can last months, the Physical Batterer will repeat the same behavior he exhibited when they met. He may pay close attention to her, giving her gifts and showering her with love. He'll be likely to take all the blame for whatever is wrong in their partnership. She'll be thrilled with the attention and the proliferation of love. She'll make every effort to "rethink" how she views him, misinterpreting his jealousy and possessiveness as love. After all, if he is doing all this, he must be afraid to lose me, and therefore he must love me, she thinks. Starved for the male attention she missed in her childhood, and never having experienced a healthy male-female relationship, she accepts his advances and forgives him—again.

CAN ANYTHING BE DONE ABOUT PHYSICAL ABUSE?

It must be very frustrating to be a counselor in a battered women's shelter. The same women come back time after time, but each time they go back to their abusive spouses. Some end up in jail for killing their spouses, and some end up dead themselves. The amazing thing is that no matter what you tell them, what you do, or what fifty million other people tell them, some women just won't leave. Somehow, the relationship is like a drug for these women.

The battered woman always has a reason why she must return. She has to go back home for financial reasons. Besides, he didn't beat her as badly as he could have. She loves (is obsessed with) him. Or maybe he threatened to kill himself, or her, or the kids, or her parents if she didn't go back. He says he will never beat her again, and he really means it this time.

Sure. He would climb the highest mountain, ford the widest stream. Because he loves her? No. Because if that is what it takes to get back control of her, he will do it.

There is a very low rehabilitation rate for Physical Batterers. Not only is there a lack of rehabilitation facilities, there is also an initial lack of interest on the part of the Batterers to participate in rehabilitation. The Physical Batterer believes that he wouldn't beat his wife if she didn't get him upset. He needs more than a few months of psychotherapy. If he's going to change, he has to rethink the way he approaches life, and that's a very hard—and very scary—thing to do.

WHAT TO DO

I believe that the Physical Batterer really can't help himself. He is out of control, just replaying some old tapes in his head and using the people in his life as players to act out his drama, all the while rationalizing his actions.

Most of us rationalize the same way. For example, the employee who feels he or she is being taken for granted takes home (steals) pencils and paper from the office. Stealing office supplies makes the employee feel less like a victim. By "taking something back," the employee may feel more in control of the work situation.

We also rationalize negative things *other* people do, usually because we want to feel there's a "reason" for his or her actions, an excuse. But quite often, the only way to excuse someone else's reprehensible behavior is to take the blame oneself. The battered wife tells herself that if she hadn't burnt the spaghetti, she wouldn't have gotten a beating. This helps her to *feel* in control of her life, but not to *be* in control of it. When we hear one of our neighbors had a heart attack, we sigh with relief when we find out that he had been under a lot of stress or that his diet was poor. Why? Because we like to think that if he had controlled his diet, he would not have had the heart attack. Well, folks, s#%+ happens. While there are many things we can do to control our lives, there are also many things we are powerless over. (And we're probably afraid to admit it.) A lightning bolt that strikes you has no animosity toward you; it is just being a lightning bolt. The man who beats his wife is similar to that lightning bolt. He is the way he is, and, if he can't strike you, he'll strike someone or something else. *But the thing getting struck does not have to be you!* You *can* end physical abuse, by leaving.

I'm sure you've read what follows before, but take the time now to read it again.

God, grant me the serenity to accept the things I cannot change,
the courage to change the things I can,
and the wisdom to know the difference.

You cannot stop a man from beating you unless you physically remove yourself. It's that simple. If you don't want to be hit by lightning, you've got to move away from the storm. There is help for this man if he seeks it, but *you* can't help him.

4

Let's Talk

So far, we have explored misunderstandings between men and women. We have exposed the intricacies of nasty men by putting them into five categories and generalizing about them. Perhaps, in reading the preceding chapters, you have realized that your man is not so bad after all or that your man is very similar to one, if not all, of these men.

Before you read any further, it's time for us to have a little talk.

The rest of this book (if you follow it in sequence) contains some very powerful concepts. These ideas have been around for ages; I am presenting them to you in a way that is adapted to relationships. I must warn you that if you expose yourself to these perspectives, your life could change. Continuing to read may be a bit like opening Pandora's box, except that in the long run it can be very good for you. You may not like everything you learn here. There is no such thing as being tactful with some of these perspectives. You may change your frame of reference and transform into an entirely different person. I am just giving you fair warning.

Ready? Just start with an open mind. Take a deep breath, and leave your current methods of thinking about life at the period at the end of this sentence. There. You can come back and pick them up later if you want to.

Let's go.

REALITY

Suppose you have a new man in your life and you think he is great, maybe even "the one." At the same time, many of your friends, whose opinions you trust, think he is a real jerk. What is the reality here? Is he a frog or a prince? It is all a matter of perspective. You are operating from a different "reality" than your friends.

WHAT IS REALITY, REALLY?

There are three kinds of reality.

Societal Reality

Societal reality includes the two types of realities that society (or the majority of it) subscribes to: physical reality and agreement reality. *Physical reality* is when a rock hits you in the head. The rock doesn't care if you think it should hit you in the head. It doesn't care if you believe in its existence. It will still fall on your head if you happen to be standing underneath it when it falls. A rock is not fair, and it can put a dent in your head. Its behavior simply follows the laws of physics, not what we believe a rock should do.

If our beliefs align perfectly with the laws of physics, then we get to be right and to anticipate the behavior of a rock. However, some of us believe that a rock couldn't possibly fall on us and then feel unfairly treated when it does. It may be enlightening for us to know how we come to be standing where the rocks fall.

Agreement reality is simply agreement. Marriage exists only because everyone *agrees* it does. If you lived in a culture where all males and females who lived together were considered married, you would not be able to live with a person of the opposite sex and call yourself unmarried without going against reality. A rose is beautiful only if everyone agrees it is. A roach is disgusting only if we all agree it is.

Whenever you go against physical reality or agreement reality, you will get resistance. Because of physical reality, you can't expect to walk through a brick wall. By exactly the same token, if the agreement reality is that men and women who live together are married and you live with someone of the opposite sex . . . you are married, and you will be treated like you are married whether you like it or not and whether you believe it or not. Agreement reality is just as powerful as physical reality.

If the management where you work agrees that arriving late is a sign of laziness and irresponsibility, then that is the reality. It doesn't matter if you know otherwise. It doesn't matter that *you* don't agree. It doesn't matter if it's fair or not. If you come in late, the reality is that you are irresponsible and lazy. You may not like this, but that doesn't change anything. You could fight management, you could throw this book down and jump on it. You might still be fired for being late, if the reality was strong enough. No matter how right you thought you were, you would still be out of a job.

Furthermore, physical reality and agreement reality change. One minute it's sunny, the next, it's raining; one year short skirts are thought to be tacky, another, they're the height of fashion. If you do not deal with the reality at hand, you may undergo a severe reality adjustment. Problems arise when we are not familiar with the reality at hand, refuse to acknowledge it, have a false perception, or don't know what the reality's limits are.

It may be enlightening for you to know how you came to be the one that got fired.

Personal Reality

Your perception of the way things are is your personal reality. This is a combination of what you have seen in the past and what you believe to be true in the present. Because of this, your perception almost never exactly matches the external phenomena (what is going on *outside* your head). In fact, much of our lives are spent finding a comfortable balance between our personal reality and agreement reality (you can't argue much with physical reality).

Let's say that your personal reality is that you are an intelligent person. You have good credentials, and you function in an important job. Then you take a trip to the Philippines and end up in the jungle with members of the Dumagat tribe. Your societal reality then may be that you are the dumbest thing ever seen, so don't be prancing around in the jungle acting like a pompous ass. If you do, the Dumagats might not be willing to teach you how to get food for yourself. I'm sure they have a word in their vocabulary equivalent to the word *idiot*, and you just might hear that word murmured a lot, followed by gleeful laughter. Your severe reality adjustment may include the experience of hunger.

Staying in the U.S.A. won't protect you from the perils of remaining in your personal reality. We have all been embarrassed by making asses of ourselves. Sometimes such mistakes become growth experiences, teaching us a little humility.

It may be enlightening for you to know the difference between your personal reality and agreement reality.

Truth

My Webster's dictionary says truth is actuality, the quality of a thing that is exactly what it purports to be. The truth is what *is*. It is what is left over after you take away judgment, past experience, and perception, and see (not with the eyes or mind) things in present time, as they are. Given that we human beings always compare, figure, signify, and analyze everything via our personal perception, we rarely know truth in pure form.

Some people call being able to see the truth "wisdom."

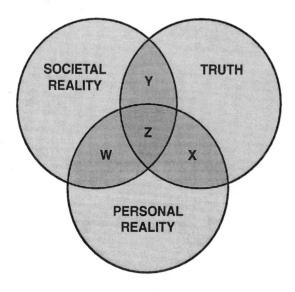

The Big Picture

Personal reality: This is what you perceive. Notice that there are some areas of truth that are not within your perception, as well as some areas of societal reality (agreement and physical) that are not within your perception.

Societal reality: This is what is believed by the world or a group that you may encounter, such as citizens of a country or members of a religion (a Christian's reality is different from a Muslim's, for example). Note the part of your personal reality which is not agreed upon and which is also not truth.

Truth: The truth is what is so, whether you or anyone else believes it. Notice the area of truth that is not within our reality. These are truths that are undiscovered as yet.

Now let's explain the areas where the circles intersect.

W: In this area are instances in which you and everyone else believe that something is so, but it is not the truth. If you lived back in Pasteur's time, you and the rest of society may not have believed Pasteur when he said there were little germs crawling all over your body, yet it was true.

This area also represents the instances in which you and others share a mind-set. For example, you meet a frog. He is dressed up like a prince. You believe he is a prince and so do your friends . . . but he is a frog.

X: This is the area where you could end up after you marry the frog. It is still true that he is a frog, and you have come to realize it (in your personal reality), but everyone else still thinks he is a prince.

Y: In this area, the circumstances are, for example, that everyone knows the guy you are with is a frog, and it is true, but you are so infatuated that this just doesn't fit your personal reality.

Z: In this area falls the occasion on which you see him as a frog, he is a frog, and everyone else sees that he is a frog. It's true, you believe it, and everyone else believes it too.

This perspective on societal reality, personal reality, and truth can give people the ability to discriminate between the divisions of reality, thereby enabling them to deal with agreement reality (regardless of whether agreement reality is right or wrong).

Through this perspective, schizophrenics are able to function. They begin to understand, for example, that even though they may hear voices coming out of the sidewalk, other people don't, and they had better not mention the voices to other people. By the same token, the person who is often late for work had better start getting to work on time or have an excuse that fits the reality (what management believes), or she may not have a job.

The world's reality is not necessarily fair, and you may not like it, but it helps to know where you stand. In case you hadn't noticed, the world is not the way it *should* be, it *is* the way it *is*.

ACCEPTANCE

Many of us have trouble accepting certain things. If a man cannot accept some of his emotions, he goes into denial (of his feelings). A woman may not be able to accept that she cannot change her husband, so she harbors false hope. At some point, all of us are faced with some reality that we do not want to accept. Two of the biggest underlying factors in nonacceptance are the fear that acceptance means that we agree with the rightness of the thing we are accepting and the fear of powerlessness that may go along with acceptance.

First of all, to accept that something exists does not mean that you agree with it. Learning more about it does not mean you agree with it either. In the case of physical reality (gravity, weather, and so on), you can get as irate about it as you like. You can wish really hard for it to be different. You can refuse to accept it. You can refuse to believe it exists. It will *still* affect you. For example, you are powerless over the laws of physics. But by accepting the laws of physics and learning about them, you can change the way you interact with the physical world; you can stop hoping, denying, and wishing, and instead do things that won't waste your energy and that will give you something in return. You can build a house to keep out the wind, or you can put up lightning rods for lightning, whereas *no* amount of wishing or hoping will help you solve your weather problems.

The same is true for other realities. Things are not always the way they should be, could be, or would be. They *are* the way they *are*. The Liar will make promises to you about how it *will* be. The Cro-Magnon glimmers with potential, the way he *can* be. The Verbal Batterer and Physical Batterer will say they are sorry and tell you what they *shouldn't have* done. These are all just promises, hope, and potential. At the moment he is caught in a damaging lie, the Liar truly wants to change. The Don Juan truly wants to settle down with one woman (as soon as he meets his soul mate). The Physical Batterer is truly sorry after he beats you up. But the way they *are* is the way they *are*. Just because the Liar tells you he will change does not make him something other than a Liar. If he lies, he is a Liar. If he beats you up, he is a Batterer. And by not accepting the simple truth at hand, we deprive ourselves of taking the first step toward dealing with these things.

I have learned that I am powerless over chocolate. Before I accepted that fact, I would tell myself the type of things that all chocoholics tell themselves. "One won't hurt," "Well, one more won't hurt," "Ah, what the hell. I'll exercise it off," "There's only a couple left. I may as well finish the bag," ad nauseam.

It wasn't that I was powerless all the time. Most of the time I could resist. But it only takes five minutes out of a twenty-four-hour day to devour a box of chocolates. Keeping them in the house "in case we have company" would guarantee that they would be gone within twenty-four hours. Then I would feel remorse for doing what I said I wouldn't do. I would always make an honest-to-God promise to myself that I would not eat any the next day.

Admitting that I was powerless does not mean that I gave up trying and just ate all the chocolate in sight. It meant that I accepted that I cannot eat chocolate without eating a lot of it, because I am addicted to it. I can't keep it in the house. I can't take that first bite, because I would pig out on it later or the next day. Other people I know have no problem with chocolate and can eat it whenever they want, but for me it causes a weight problem and the mental problem of obsessing over it. By deciding not to have any—ever—I gave up all my thoughts about it, such as whether it was fair that I couldn't have any, whether my turning it down would offend someone who offered it to me, and the ungenerous feeling I had when I actually did have company and resentfully offered my stash of chocolate to them. Only after I admitted I was powerless over chocolate did I begin to take responsibility for my problem. This may sound paradoxical. But my acceptance of my problem was exactly like an alcoholic admitting he is powerless over alcohol. He then stays away from bars (I stay away from the candy aisle at the supermarket). He knows he can't take that first drink (I know I can't take that first bite). My problem became solvable only when I realized it had nothing to do with weight loss, nutrition, or willpower . . . just knowing my limits.

In summary
1. I had to accept what I could not change (my susceptibility to chocolate, the weight gain that would result if I ate

chocolate, that people would continue to offer me chocolate, and that even though I could work it off, I wouldn't).

2. I had to change the things I could (no chocolate in the house, no walks down the candy aisle, no chocolate even if it meant offending someone).

3. I had to develop the wisdom to determine what I could and couldn't change. (I could not delude myself that it would be all right to have just one or blame the person offering me chocolate.) I had to face my reality vis à vis chocolate.

4. I had to take responsibility for it. This is a big one. Read on.

RESPONSIBILITY

When I give seminars on relationships, I devote a whole night to the subject of responsibility. After a woman took one of my classes on responsibility she said, "You opened my eyes to a lot of things I really needed to know." Then she smiled with a twinkle in her eye and said, "You bastard."

First, let's distinguish between *responsibility* and *blame*. Responsibility is *not* blame. If a hurricane hits, I am not to blame for it, but I can take responsibility for it by helping the individuals who were hurt by it. That is easy to see, huh?

OK. Now, what if I was driving my car out of the parking lot and I hit you with my car, breaking both your legs? Who is responsible for that? If I pay your hospital bills and reimburse you for your loss of pay, have I taken total responsibility for your injury? The answer is no. Who gets to feel the pain? Who has to go to the hospital? No matter what I do or what I say, you are responsible for your injury. Yes, I am to blame.

Some people have hang-ups left over from their childhoods, and they blame their parents for their problems. Yes, maybe their parents are to blame. But, who *has* the hang-up? Who has to deal with it? Who is really responsible for the hang-up? Even if society says your parents are responsible for your hang-ups, that is only agreement reality and not necessarily the truth.

If someone shoots you, who is responsible for it? Right! You are! If someone beats you, invalidates you, or hurts you in any way, who is responsible? That's right, *you* are.

So what I am getting at here is the possibility that you are responsible for everything that happens to you, no matter what you believe, no matter whether you like it or not, no matter if it is fair or not, and no matter what the agreement reality says.

Doesn't that just make your day? And aren't you glad you picked up this book? Well, hold on to this perspective for a while longer; it can only get better now.

You see, we are really foolish sometimes. We *allow* bad things to happen to us as long as these things are not our fault. Some people get into cars with drunk drivers, but think, if they get into an accident, at least it won't be their fault. Wow, some compensation! Others get into relationships and do their best, so if it doesn't turn out, at least it won't be their fault. Again, wow, some compensation!

Taking responsibility for or ownership of a situation can be a powerful experience. In my own life, I went through a period where I was bothered by invalidation. I unknowingly allowed my invalidator to make me feel so bad about myself that I would look to her to make all my decisions. For a long time I tried to emotionally separate myself from this situation, to avoid the escalating conflict. But I didn't realize I was being invalidated because this person's exaggerations matched the degree to which I was critical of myself. So, my approach was to try to better myself as an individual so I would be beyond reproach. No sooner would I improve in one aspect than five more "honest" criticisms would come my way . . . five more things about myself I had to change. I became so overwhelmed with the task of self-change that I was ready to give up and just succumb to being the lacking character I saw myself to be. Then I had a great insight.

Most people had a high opinion of me. It was only this one person who seemed to be fixated on my negative traits. Following this insight, I heaped a lot of blame on the invalidator, but still no improvement. The invalidation didn't stop, and I continued to blame someone else for what was happening to me.

Then I remembered a problem I had handled at work. (Just follow me on this.) The people who worked for me on second shift were having problems getting information *from* the first shift and getting information *to* the third shift. The people on first shift all took off for the sitting room as soon as my second-shift people arrived. At the end of the evening, third shift would come in and hang out by the coffee machine until it was time for second shift to leave. The shifts were not talking to each other and things were not getting done properly due to the lack of communication.

I held a department meeting and I told my people I was making them 100 percent responsible for getting information and 100 percent responsible for giving information. They had to make sure they *got* it and *gave* it. In addition, each individual was responsible for making sure it happened for everybody else. They thought I was asking for the impossible, but after that, someone from second shift would go into the sitting room to intercept the first shift to ask what tasks needed to be done. At night, someone from second shift would intercept people from third shift at the coffee machines to tell them what needed to be done. They documented their conversations in a log. They were now 100 percent responsible, and there were no more communication problems after that.

So I decided that I was 100 percent responsible for the invalidation in my life. Bam! Transformation! I was choosing to take responsibility for something I was already responsible for anyway.

Invalidation, after all, was out there and it was my choice whether I was going to be passive and let it continue to happen or be active in nipping it in the bud. I wasn't taking *blame* for it. I was simply willing to take *ownership* of it. I could then ask the question, "What might I be doing that allows this to happen?" Allowing does not mean wanting. Responsibility does not mean blame. I *confronted* invalidation instead of distancing myself from it or giving in to it. I was then willingly involved. I was then a more powerful person.

So here it is: It is not your fault that the guy you fell for treated you poorly, played around on you, or was a schmuck. You are not to blame. But you *are* responsible. He hurt you because you let him. The frog is now in your life, and now you can choose to be responsible for his being there by setting limits or getting him out.

Once you realize that you are responsible for everything that happens to you, you may feel more powerless over things, but you are actually more in control. You are less inclined to let things happen to you. You are less inclined to arrogantly shake your derriere at the lightning bolts of life. You begin to realize that the lightning bolt doesn't care whether you believe that it never strikes the same place twice. It will unfairly charbroil your rump no matter what you think, because it is just being a lightning bolt. If you really understand this, there is less of a chance I will find you indignantly rubbing your smoking bottom. The fact is that you end up taking responsibility for things anyway, just like you breathe anyway. It's a cosmic joke.

5

Jennifer: A Love Story

This little chapter is about a woman who became *realistic* about her problem, *accepted* it, and *took responsibility* for it. Doing so changed her life.

A good friend of mine (whom I will call Jennifer) had moved to the area where I live to be near her boyfriend (whom I will call Bob), whom she hoped to marry. He had not proposed, but he had talked about marriage and children from a personal, philosophical perspective, and he had taken her to look at houses a few times. Because of his actions and words, she assumed that he saw marriage in his future.

They had been seeing each other for two years and they had become closer and closer. They loved and cared for each other.

One day, they were looking through an appliance store and Jennifer noticed a VCR that she liked. She remarked about the new features it had, and Bob said he would buy it for her for her birthday. She became upset. He already had a VCR—why would he want to buy another if they were going to be living in the same house? This made her think that he had little intention of marrying her and that he was leading her on. She accused him of this, as well as of being noncommittal. The more she thought about it, the more upset she became.

Now, no one likes to be nagged or belittled. But a man sometimes sees himself as being nagged when his partner just wants him to hold up his end of the relationship. A man is taught to be independent, so it is against his "enculturation" to be interdependent in a permanent, daily way. He likes having his freedom to do what he wants without having to check with someone else. There aren't many men who are actually enthusiastic about getting married when they already have a "perfect" relationship with a woman, one in which they can have her company and still remain autonomous. A man is prone to deny feelings that might lead to the demise of his independence, and he is also sometimes unaware of just how much he has to lose if his relationship is ended.

My advice to Jennifer was to stop attacking Bob, take a look at her own needs, and then present him with her needs in terms of herself alone. Men listen better when they don't feel they're being attacked.

Jennifer spoke to Bob. She told him that she loved him very much and would always remember him, no matter what. (Men love to feel special.) She would continue to see him for now (no ultimatums), but her plans for her life included marriage and children. She told him that she understood if he was not ready, but she had to move on with her life.

This made Bob realize that he could lose Jennifer and that (to add insult to injury) someone else might end up with this fine woman. It also made him realize how strongly he felt about her and how important she was in his life. Over the next few weeks, he brought her flowers, he took her to nice places, and he paid more attention to her.

The next time Jennifer spoke to me, she said, "I guess we're back," and she told me all the wonderful things Bob was doing, how loving he was, and that they had spent many intimate moments together. So I asked her, "What's changed? Isn't he the loving, caring person he always was?"

"Well, yes," she said.

"So, what goal does Bob have? Men like to have a goal, you know. I think he already accomplished his goal; he has you back. Did you change any of your goals in life since we talked last?"

"No," she said.

I made her realize that nothing had changed, but that a man is very easy to deal with if you realize what his perspective is and if you can speak to him in terms he will understand. I suggested to her that she let Bob know that she appreciated how sweet he had been in the last weeks and that she had thoroughly enjoyed his company, but that she didn't want him to think her goals in life had changed. She needed to tell him that she still intended to get on with her life in a way that was meaningful to her and also that she understood that he was probably not ready for marriage and she could respect him for that.

I asked her if that was the way she really felt or whether she was content with things the way they were. I thought that if she really did want marriage and Bob didn't, she would be ending it sooner or later anyway, so she would be better off addressing the issue then. But she must say this to Bob only if she really meant it; she could not do it to manipulate him into marrying her. She had to be "willing" to lose him.

After thinking about it, she told him once again that she needed to move forward, because she really did feel that way.

Now Bob had the information he needed to make his decision. Jennifer wasn't nagging him. She wasn't berating him. He understood her goals in life, and he still felt he had a special place in her life. He also realized that he would be a fool to let her go. He asked her to marry him.

Now, it worked out well for both Bob and Jennifer, but even if he had chosen *not* to marry her, it would have worked out for her in the long run. So, let's review her approach.

1. She saw the problem as hers, not his. Therefore she didn't try to change him. She accepted him for the way he was, not the way he could be, should be, or would be.

2. She considered changing herself or changing her relationship. She decided that she was not going to change herself (her goals, her plans), so she planned the first moves toward changing her relationship with Bob by speaking to him frankly about her goals, all the while accepting the distinct possibility her relationship with him might have to end.

As for Bob, he accepted himself the way he was because Jennifer accepted him the way he was. In order to change, a person has to accept himself the way he is. It may sound paradoxical, but if you don't accept yourself exactly the way you are, then you can't change, because in order to change you have to change *from* something. If you don't accept what that something is, then you are doomed to stay the same.

Bob told himself that he didn't want to get married, but deep down he really *did* want to. This was just another case of a woman making a man see the way he really feels by doing what she needs to do to get her own life on track.

6

Transforming Him

You can't transform anyone. Now, in case you didn't get that
last sentence, let me say it again in bolder type. **You can't
transform anyone.** Yes, that's right—you, the person reading this book—no matter how special you are, no matter
how much love you have to give, no matter what you have
accomplished in your life, you cannot transform *anyone*. No,
not even him.

I know that there are women who will read this book
from cover to cover and then run off with guys who are
going to make their lives hell on earth. They think they can
use the information in this book to change their favorite
Cro-Magnons, Liars, or Don Juans. Well, there are thousands of women out there who have tried to "improve" their
men. They can verify what I am telling you. But you think to
yourself that was them, and this is me. Do you think you are
so special that you can do what God won't do? It is very
important for you to understand that you can't transform
your nasty man. You must give up this approach before you
run out of gas. Too many women who have tried have experienced the "empty tank syndrome," and it is no fun. Worse,
you've got the empty tank, and the car is still in the drive-
way

As a man, I am telling you that you cannot change a man. You can only take responsibility for what you need in your life. Trying to change someone is manipulation. He will feel it and know it and he won't feel accepted when you do it.

Take a look at your man. Whatever it is about him you want to be different, you can instead expect to have more of the same later. If he drinks now, he won't stop drinking after you are married or after you have your first child. He may drink more. He won't be happier, won't treat you any better, be more responsible, or stop going out with the boys. Contrary to popular belief, love is not a catalyst for changes like these.

What you see is what you get, no matter what promise he makes to you and how much he means it. Otherwise, you must make your decision about him based on what you see in front of you, and potential doesn't count. We all have potential. Those who are using their potential are using it, and those who are not *are not*. There are things you *can* do, but only after you fully accept what I have said about trying to transform others.

1. You can change yourself.
2. You can change your relationship with the frog.
3. If your frog seems truly willing to become a prince (although most frogs who are "willing" are just being manipulative) you can create an environment that is conducive to transformation.

Changing yourself means adapting a different frame of reference—seeing yourself differently, identifying a new intent or purpose for your life, starting anew without the baggage of your past, for example.

Changing your relationship means ending it *as it is*. Ending it is ending it, and that is obvious, but what is not so obvious is that changing it is ending it, and then beginning anew. On more than one occasion, I have said to someone close to me, "Our relationship is not working. I want to end it." Then I continue, "I still want to have a relationship with you, but not the one we have." Eventually, we redefine our relationship, or rather, define the new relationship. Long-term relationships usually end and begin a lot. The next chapter contains tips for changing your relationship.

I know you may have liked it when I said you could create an environment for your frog to transform into a prince. The enabler-type woman breathed a sigh of relief because she could see herself nurturing her little frog through his transformation, after which he would be forever grateful and indebted to her and would never want to leave such a lovely, dedicated, and loyal person. Be careful! You have to be tough! You have to be totally willing to kick the guy out the door if he reverts to his froggy ways. There are to be no excuses. He doesn't get to lose control of himself tempo-rarily. If he's being a frog he gets treated that way. This is the only course that allows him to pick the responsibility up himself.

If a little boy came up to you with a bat and threatened to hit you with it, you probably wouldn't cower and say, "No, no! Don't hit me with the bat!" If you did, he just might hit you. Instead, you would probably say, "You put that bat down right now! Do you hear me?!" When a frog is acting like a frog, you treat him like a frog. And even when a prince is acting like a frog, you treat him like a frog.

WHAT IS TRANSFORMATION LIKE?

No one goes through a transformation kicking and scream-ing, because transformation is something you have to want before it can happen to you.

It is not behavior that indicates transformation. A selfish person who begins doing things for others is only changing his behavior. A basically self-centered person knows he needs to prove himself by changing what others think of him, whereas an unselfish person just has to be himself and improve. An unselfish person may do things that hurt others, but he is merely making mistakes, and you can expect an improvement. Many frogs *won't* make mistakes at all because they're trying to change your perception of them rather than effecting real change in their hearts (which is much harder).

A transformation is simply a shift in a man's frame of reference. No voice from heaven calls down to confirm it. No one is going to stamp his forehead or take away his individuality or force him into anything. But he will have to be a pioneer. There may be some arrows. Your man may do the very same things he did before . . . except for different reasons or in a new light. His responsibility level will rise and (believe it or not) doing the right thing will take less effort because he won't be fighting himself. It isn't succumbing, surrendering, or accepting with complacency. If he is doing that, he is not transforming. No, a transformation is when he is just riding the horse in the direction it was already going. Once transformed, he can guide the horse where he wants it to go. Men (and women) who merely pretend to change often end up sitting in a manure pile in the pasture of life all by themselves, feeling sorry for themselves and wondering what happened.

He can't do this for anyone but himself.

Many times a man's transformation begins at the point where he realizes his frame of reference is not functional or optimally functional. This may only happen after his life is a shambles. Perhaps you have finally put your foot down and he has realized that his personal reality is not getting him anywhere and that he is going to lose you.

A preferable and less painless way to change is for people to begin to take charge of their own personal growth and to learn more about themselves and life.

A counseling client of mine wanted to transform himself

after he became a father. The man had suffered some physical abuse from his own father, and he was having a hard time restraining himself from beating his own son. My client swore he would never abuse his son and had not as yet done so, but he was having a great deal of trouble containing the rage he felt at times toward his three-year-old. He was afraid it would get worse.

We discussed that his fathering "tapes" were not good. His father had been very distant, yet controlling and suppressive. I suggested that his whole father frame of reference was irreparable and that he should abandon it. He should not think of himself as the child's father, as that would trigger the old negative role-playing. He might instead think of himself simply as an older, more experienced person who could be of help to this younger, less able person until the child could fend for himself. I also suggested he read *The Prophet* (by Kahlil Gibran) on children.

The next time I saw my client, he was transformed. He said he realized that his children were not *his*, but *of him*. They were his equals, albeit with less experience than he. It was his responsibility (having brought them into this world) to give them *their* lives, not *his* life. He would stand by them through the dawn of their awakening and learn from them as they would learn from him.

How do I know this man was truly transformed? That was seventeen years ago. He never abused his son, and the impulses to do so died out with the old frame of reference as he developed his new frame of reference. He said his old fathering "tapes" have a lifetime of cobwebs on them from lack of use. His son, however, has great fathering "tapes." The abuse in this man's family, which had gone on for many generations, was now at an end.

Of course, some people never hit bottom. They hold tightly to their personal frames of reference and reality, becoming road kills on the highway of life (and taking others with them).

7

Standing Up

It may appear that I am being too tough on the men I have described in this book. After all, even the meanest guys can be affectionate, can be good providers, and can be fun to be with sometimes. And I know that many of them have come from abusive households or have grown up in adverse conditions. I have a great deal of compassion for guys who realize their behavior is dysfunctional and are really trying to change, and I hope they have a loving, understanding environment in which to undertake this difficult task. But I do *not* feel compassion for the abusive man who is in denial and doesn't want to know how he hurts others. I have no compassion for the taker who is not trying to better himself and who lives off the goodwill and pain of others. I do not feel sorry for the manipulative, self-pitying crybaby he becomes when his abusive ways do not work.

I do not have a vendetta against nasty men. I just know that enabling them is the worst thing we can do for them. Pampering them and making excuses for them will just keep them stuck in their abusive ways. As long as they get what they want through abuse, others suffer. And the women who enable these men are doing themselves and their men (as well as their children) an injustice.

Men, too, are enablers for other men. Men seem to have a live-and-let-live mentality when it comes to other men. Men are raised to be individuals, and they develop their individual-selves to be autonomous and to respect the autonomy of other men. However, I would like to see men take on a more responsible role and become more involved. When a man beats his wife and another man listens to the Batterer's justification for the act without saying it's *not* OK, he is silently condoning the behavior (and not being a real friend). When the Don Juan cheats on his wife, another man should not pretend that it's cool. He could be a better friend to the Don Juan if he said something like, "You know, you have a nice wife and family. I would really hate to see you mess that up."

If there were no enablers, there would be no invalidators. If no one put up with a nasty man's abuse, he would be terribly lonely. He might seek help with his problem, but only after he had alienated both family and friends. It is rare that a truly nasty man changes, because he is not motivated to change. It seems that there is always *someone* who is willing to put up with the abuse. But that someone does not have to be you.

MAKE A DECISION

If you're involved with an invalidator, you'll be much better off if you examine your situation and your options and decide how to handle your problems. Too many of us put off deciding anything; but as they say, "not to decide is to decide." Living with or putting up with invalidation day after day and waffling about what to do is deciding to accept the status quo. These painful days, added together, are the sum of your life. Make a decision today. And if it's not going to be today, then when? Mark a date on your calendar.

Deciding About a One-Percenter

If you are connected to an invalidator who is a true one-percenter, someone who has no conscience, and he has power over you, get him out of your life. If he is invalidating you privately, make it public, or threaten to. Be sure you have a safe backup. If I worked for Hitler and then I read this book, I would start planning my escape as soon and as covertly as possible. Everyone in league with Hitler would probably call me a deserter and a traitor. Maybe a lot of people who didn't know him would think I was paranoid, and maybe I would be unsure of myself after having been around him so long. I would try to think of what life was like was before I met him. Was I paranoid then? Was I uncertain then? Could things be any worse? If I came up with three nos to those questions, I would soon be gone.

There is a saying that you can't run away from your problems. You really can't, but you can get out of the way of other people's problems.

Deciding About a Ten-Percenter

If you are involved with an invalidator who is a ten-percenter, you have a tough row to hoe if you want to stay with him. It is likely that his childhood was filled with suppressive behavior. He will probably always display abusive behavior to some degree or another. The degree to which he consciously chooses to behave abusively is the degree to which he is evil.

There are periods of stress in anyone's life, and your nasty man may regress to abusive behavior during these times. His view of life and his experiences in life do not make him a good candidate for therapy. It is very difficult for him to open himself up to change because, first of all, he often

doesn't know who he is; second, because he probably has
not had good experience surrendering himself to an authority figure or a significant other, and he is incapable of the
kind of trust that is needed. If both his parents were unde-
pendable, he began relying on himself very early in life, and
it is difficult for him to respect anyone else.

At this time, there is not much that can be done for him.
We are close, though. When twelve-step abusers' groups
become as common as Alcoholics Anonymous, there will be
more hope. There are, of course, a lot of people in the
mental health field and other helping fields that would like
to think anything is possible. There are thousands of theo-
ries around that sound very good on paper, but if you take
a closer look you see things differently. There also need to
be more laws that force abusers into therapy. Many abusers
are incapable of volunteering for therapy, but when forced
into it, they often improve.

If you want to stay in his life in the most comfortable way
(which won't be that comfortable), you will have to become
his authority figure at those times when he is out of control
and abusive. You may have to treat him like a six-year-old,
and say things like, "Don't talk to me that way!" You will
have to position yourself to have an edge on him. For example: threaten to tell his mother or expose him publicly if he
continues his abusive behavior. Actually, there is part of him
who *is* that child, who needs limits to his behavior. You will
need to have the edge to *enforce* these limits but still be his
equal, his companion, when he is not behaving abusively.
You will have to be what he perceives as stronger than he is,
and you will have to demand respect from him. If you run
away, act scared, or beg for mercy, he will consider you
weak. You must see yourself as more capable than he is.

When he is behaving abusively, he probably will not respond to love and understanding, but even the worst crim-
inals respond to unwavering demands for respect. As long as
you are strong, it may work out. But if I were you, I would

have a backup environment for when I was not feeling up to the challenge or for when he was totally out of control.

Deciding About a Twenty-Percenter

If you are connected to a twenty-percenter, you have seen him do some very manipulative things or start to but then catch himself. His intent is not evil. He (like some of the other guys in this book) probably has trouble letting out his feelings in healthy ways. He tries to suppress his feelings until they get to be too much, and he loses control and does or says something stupid. Don't take it personally; it is probably repressed rage that he feels toward the person who suppressed him in the past. Or he is just acting out some of the behavior he has witnessed.

Try to just let the moment pass without antagonizing him, defending yourself, or snowballing the argument. Later, when his rage has passed, talk about it. Do *not* forget it and just let it go. That sends a nonverbal message to him that all he has to do to get his own way is have a temper tantrum. If he flies into a rage every time you gently confront him, maybe he is a ten-percenter.

You may realize after reading this book that the man you love, are attached to, or are obsessed with is not going to change for your sake or for anyone else's and that he is not someone you want in your life anymore. If you have read everything so far and still can't decide whether to disconnect from him or not, then it probably doesn't matter what decision you make. Flip a coin. If it's heads, he stays, if it is tails, he goes. This is a secret technique of many prominent executives. Because sometimes it doesn't matter what decision you make, as long as you make one. Then you just stick to it, having confidence in your having brought about the outcome.

IF YOUR LIFE WITH HIM GIVES YOU
MORE PAIN THAN JOY

Even if you know that he has to go, you may not feel strong enough to get him out of your life. Do it anyway; line up others to support you. Most people underestimate the strength they have. So many women find that their men try to put them into a double bind. You must realize that your abuser has worked diligently to undermine your confidence. He may threaten to do terrible things to himself, to you, to your parents, and even to your children if you do not come back to him. You may be so emotionally exhausted that you succumb to him and return to the most dangerous situation of all. If he is threatening to do terrible things, it stands to reason that he has less of an opportunity to do them if you are not in his presence. (Despite all the publicity "stalkers" receive, the statistics are much worse for physically abused women who go back home versus those who stay away.) Find someone who has been through a similar experience and has succeeded in dealing with it. Line up your reserves and then go all the way.

Sometimes a woman does not want to appear wrong. She does not want to be the one to leave. She may be afraid that people will think she is a bitch, a whore, or a bad mother. I knew a woman who had lived with a Verbal Batterer for twelve years. Her self-esteem had never been lower. She had stress-related physical problems (colitis, ulcers). Most people thought he was a nice guy. He was more sociable than she was and made friends with ease. She was afraid all her friends would shun her if she left. (He had discouraged her from making friends to whom *she* could relate.) She was sure his family would reject her, and was afraid even her own family would disown her. They didn't really know of the abuse she was subjected to, and they thought the two had a good marriage. They thought he was supportive of her (helping her with her illnesses) and that he was good with the kids. (He would often remind her of her family's perception.)

In counseling she asked me why she couldn't bring herself to leave him. I told her that if she left, the agreement reality might be that she was a bitch, a whore, and maybe even a bad mother. That is, though she was not any of these things, she would have to be willing to be perceived that way by others, or she would never leave.

She finally left. When she did, a great sense of relief came over her. She had tough financial problems, and there were people who rejected her and thought badly of her. But she said she realized she could deal with all those problems. In fact, during this period, her ulcers and colitis subsided. She said she felt almost proud to be viewed as a bitch. It gave her a lot of power. She was able to see who her friends really were. Her family, who were philosophically against divorce, did not criticize her once. In fact, her father said to her, "In case you hadn't noticed, I haven't said anything to you about your divorce. I am still philosophically opposed to divorce, but at the same time, I can't understand how you put up with that bastard for as long as you did." (Apparently her father had not wanted to cause dissension, so he hadn't said anything while she was married to him.) Her sister-in-law (ex-husband's sister) saw her in the supermarket, walked over to her, and said, "I just want you to know I understand."

OK. So now you have flipped a coin and become willing to be a bitch. (Crazy book, isn't it? People who happened to read this section first would really be confused.) But there is one more item to cover. (No, I'm not going to tell you how to choose a divorce lawyer. There are plenty of resources available once you have made that tough decision.) The next topic is grieving.

The death of the dream about who he could have been can be just as devastating as the death of a person. You may have to go through all the processes of grieving for the relationship, saying goodbye, and getting on with your life. Worse, you may have to do it without the supports our culture and society have set up for widows (funerals, words of comfort, sympathy). These supports allow and even encourage the widow to be passive in her hour of grief. *You* are going to have to go after what *you* need . . . asking favors, doing research, being kind to yourself. If you were in great pain putting up with this guy's abuse, doing these things will be easier to deal with, and after a while it can get much better. If you had no potential for a happier life with him . . . now you can see the light at the end of the tunnel. It's the difference between wandering around (feeling indecision, hoping, wishing) and having a direction.

IF YOU THINK YOU CAN WORK IT OUT

Having made it this far in the book, you may realize that your man isn't really that bad after all. (You can breath a sigh of relief!) Maybe he is just a little selfish or self-absorbed, and perhaps you have realized that you are enabling him to act this way, maybe even expecting him to. In that case, put your foot down and tell him how you expect to be treated. (If he has seen this book lying around, he probably has a sense that the jig is up, anyway.) But also realize that this man—each man—is just a man, with plenty of human shortcomings. You may need to mourn for that perfect man you will never meet and into whom your man will never change. If you are really being hurt by your illusions, maybe you will settle for one of us decent, imperfect guys. Just make sure it's one of us who has your best interests at heart.

All this reminds me of a story about a Christmas tree, which goes something like this: Once upon a time there was a person who was looking for a perfect Christmas tree. She went to every Christmas tree lot in the city and could not find one. Finally, she settled for one that was good but not perfect. She took it home and spent hours decorating it carefully and with love. After she had decorated it, a tree salesperson called and said that a perfect Christmas tree had just arrived on the lot. She rushed down to see it, and sure enough, it was perfect. She thought about the Christmas tree at home, and then looked at the bare, perfect Christmas tree. She said, "No thanks. I have *my* Christmas tree at home."

The moral is this: You can't always have what you want, but you *can* want what you have. If you hold back giving a man that last special bit of your heart because you are waiting for a prince, you will die holding on to it. If he is a decent guy, love him completely . . . anyway . . . because he is *yours*.

Now, if you have decided that you are going to keep your man, you will probably want to overcome some of the negative qualities he has that are what made you pick up this book in the first place. I don't like to give pat answers to problems. A good psychologist doesn't tell you what to do. He or she acts as a catalyst for you to realize what your options are and for you to gain insight into yourself and others so that you can pick the direction you are going in and make your own decisions and plans. I could demand that a battered woman leave her husband, and she may absolutely not leave. But the insight she gains into herself (and him) may assist her in dealing with him and decrease the incidents of abuse.

I know one woman who was successful in stopping her abuser. She hit him in the head with an iron frying pan, knocking him unconscious. When he woke up he couldn't remember the incident, but he did not physically abuse her afterward, and from then on he showed her respect. So is that the solution for everyone? Well, OK then, just go out and purchase a seven-pound iron skillet from your nearest department store. (Obviously, you *should not* do this!)

What I *can* do is offer suggestions and give examples of what others have done. If these examples and suggestions are not within your personality, then I suggest that you look for someone you trust who has been through a similar situation and use him or her as a mentor (no, I'm not going to give you the telephone number of the frying pan lady).

Pick the Subject

Pick *one* thing you would like to see change about your man. Make sure it is something that he *can* change. Before you ask him to do something about it, bring up something you like about him (preferably something that relates to your request). Then ask him if he would be willing to make the change. Don't be afraid to ask him to do it *for you*. Men usually like to please their partners. Make sure you get him to agree to it (make it a reality). Make sure you only work on this one thing. Don't overwhelm him with so many things that he forgets the first thing you asked him to do. Offer your help. For example:

You: Honey, I know you do a lot of things around the house, and there is one more thing that I would really appreciate. Garbage days are on Tuesday and Friday, and if the garbage is not taken out, it accumulates in the garage and starts to smell. Sometimes the smell knocks me off my feet when I get out of my car. Is there any way I can help you to remember to take it out?

He: Well, you know, sometimes I have a lot on my mind, and I forget.

You: OK. How about if I remind you right after dinner on the night before? If I did, do you promise you would take it out right then?

Notice there is no blaming ("You never remember to take out the garbage"). There are no demands ("I want you to take out that damn garbage"). There is no complaining ("God! That garbage is disgusting!") There is no unfavorable comparison with others ("All the other men on the block take out their garbage on garbage day").

Start Big or Small

Should you start with your biggest beef or the smallest? I would suggest you start off with something your man is likely to be successful at. There is an inner child in everyone, and that inner child likes to succeed and be acknowledged. If your partner can feel good about himself, he will be inclined to do more.

If there is a major problem that needs to be resolved immediately, you won't be able to wait. You need to be assertive and to just say, "I can't live with this. We have got to do something." If he doesn't want to do anything, then say, "OK. *I* have got to do something."

Are you afraid to confront him because you lack confidence? Read on.

Confidence

I think there is only a subtle difference between a person who has confidence in herself and a person who is unsure of herself. I believe it is ultimately a person's choice whether she has confidence and self-esteem. A confident person is sure of her intent, and this drives her to think that her thoughts about things are correct even though other people may have a different opinion. A person who does not have confidence in herself may think she is sure of her intent, but she lets the invalidation of the past halt the driving force of her intent. She is afraid to be wrong and afraid to make mistakes. She approaches things as if she is wrong instead of right until proven otherwise. *Choose* whether you are going to be confident in yourself or not; and keep choosing. Choose confidence again and again, every time it comes up. Do not choose arrogance . . . choose simple confidence. We are born with it, and we keep it until we let someone talk us out of it.

I am angry about this. It always angers me when I see a person let someone talk, manipulate, or invalidate her out of her confidence. Sometimes it seems as if for every fine person there is a lesser human being telling the fine one she is wrong. Once you have the right intent, assume you are right. You may make some mistakes. It's OK. Pick yourself up and continue. Mistakes are just opportunities for insights that lead to improvements.

Remember that No One Deserves to Be Treated Poorly

So, you have been dumped by a Don Juan. Or maybe you have been lied to, treated with disrespect, or abused. Are you one of the people who believes that, when certain things happen to them, they must have caused it or in some way deserved it? I am all for a person's willingness to take responsibility for what happens to her and to look at what she may have done to allow it or to contribute to it. But I also realize that in this world there is an element of chance. If someone throws an egg into a crowd of people, you might be the one who experiences its cracking over your nose. Just because it happens to you doesn't mean you deserved it or caused it to happen. Sometimes what happens has more to do with the physical reality of chance, motion, and gravity.

Even the most intelligent and enlightened person can be deceived by another. But there is a big difference between "I *must* have caused it" and "I *may* have contributed to it."

A Note for Givers

Giving all of yourself is different from giving your all. Giving your all has limits. Giving all of yourself doesn't end until death.

A certain amount of selfishness is necessary for a balanced and happy life. Extreme self*ish*ness and extreme self*less*ness are obviously destructive—it is the balance that is important. If your environment is not conducive to a balance, it is time to change your environment. If you burn yourself out, no one benefits. I recommend that you be as good to yourself as you are to others.

A giver may try to balance a relationship or family by migrating to the pole opposite her selfish partner. That allows the selfish partner to be even more selfish. The selfish partner *needs* to move toward the self*less*ness pole, but won't as long as the giver is there. This situation does not help to develop the taker at all; it inhibits his growth.

An extreme giver will usually have some altruistic ideas about giving. Many times these ideas are the result of manipulation by some authority figure in the giver's past who actually imposed these concepts on the giver for the selfish purpose of controlling her and taking advantage of her. Does that make the giver a fool? It does only if nothing changes after she has read this paragraph and understood it. If you are a giver, you'd better read this paragraph again and again until you "see" what I am saying. Yes, *you*. Yes, *now*.

Sharing This Book

If you have decided that your man is not one of the nasty men in this book, you may want to share this book with him. Just make sure you tell him that you read this book and it made you appreciate him. Most men are decent human beings (even if they don't read books like this). Your partner probably knows some of the characters in this book. Also, he will undoubtedly recognize some of his own traits here and there. (We all have *some*.) Point out to him that this book was written by a man. Your guy may be able to better understand a woman's frame of reference as seen through a man's perspective.

ATTENTION, ACKNOWLEDGMENT, AFFINITY, AND ADMIRATION

What I am about to say is very important. For some people, this is the most important part of the book. Paying attention to someone, acknowledging his feelings, showing affinity to him, and admiring him are the four best, most productive ways to get his cooperation.

Paying attention, acknowledging, showing affinity, and admiring are the secrets of charisma. Making a habit of doing these things, a habit that you can develop with practice, goes beyond just being a method of dealing with nasty men. Think about it: what do you value most in human relations? If someone pays attention to you, acknowledges your feelings, likes you, and admires you . . . do you feel like invalidating the person?

Do I have to list specific things to admire about a person? If I did, your admiration wouldn't be genuine, and your efforts wouldn't work. *You* have to find something to admire about the person and then admire it. You have to observe some of the person's feelings and then acknowledge them. You have to identify something you can like about this person and then like it (show him affinity). You have to listen to the person to give him attention.

I just gave you one of the secrets of the universe. Try it. Get good at it. Get really good at it. Really mean it. Really show an interest in people, acknowledge their feelings, like them, and sincerely admire them. Do this and the world is yours, but you can't fake it. It has to be genuine. When you do these things sincerely, it is like magic. You start seeing the good in people (because that is what you focus on), and that raises people's confidence to the point where they feel OK about themselves in your presence. When people feel OK about themselves, they tend not to want to invalidate. Often people behave the way you expect them to. As Bogey might say, "Ya know what I mean, sweethaht?"

Exception

People *tend* not to invalidate someone who admires them. There are exceptions, however, such as in the case of the person who feels *so* bad about himself that he thinks if you admire him you must be worse than he is. He will punish you for helping him, because you obviously have poor judgment to admire such a lowly person as himself. Be nice to him, and he will think you are a sucker. Spit on him, and he will respect you. Be firm with this guy. Don't be afraid to say no. He is out of control, and he knows it. Treat him like a bad kid, and keep him under control (at least until you can get out of his space).

DON'T BE AFRAID OF CONFRONTING HIM

Confronting a person about what he did or said makes him take responsibility for it. It also makes him respect you. You can confront him with humor; be friendly about it. Or you can confront with anger. Do whatever you think will work best.

There was a woman married to a man whom she had to confront every three months or so. This man became the most doting husband after each confrontation, but then his respect would gradually deteriorate until she had to face off with him again. As his respectfulness waned, he would make derogatory remarks about her behind her back. If she didn't find out, he would get away with it. After he got away with it for a while, he would keep making it more obvious until she would catch him and put him in his place. A look at how this man's perception of reality affected his behavior may help you to understand people like this.

A normal pattern of behavior is as follows:

- You do something to hurt someone.
- You feel remorse (take responsibility for having done it).
- You apologize and atone.

But this man's pattern of behavior was as follows:

- He did something to hurt someone.

- Since he didn't want to (or couldn't) admit to any wrong-doing, he chose to treat her with disrespect, thinking "Anyone that would let me step on her that way must be a coward."
- He stepped on her again. It was easier when he had less respect for her.

When she confronted this man, it punished him. *She* was not punishing him; he just felt punished. That wiped the slate clean of his wrongdoing, and it made him respect her again. When he got out of control, he could not stop himself. She had to stop him.

One very important point about solutions must be reiterated here. If you think that I (or anyone else) can supply you with an exact answer or a magical solution, then you are being unrealistic. The man I just discussed had to be confronted. That was the only thing that would work with him. His wife handled him well. If you think you can deal with someone like that without confronting him, he may drive you crazy. He will keep abusing you and disrespecting you to the end. You may end up a nervous wreck, because he can't stop himself.

The man in the example above had enough redeeming value to keep his wife from wanting to leave him. I am sure it was difficult for her to deal with him. It is not fair that she had to put up with that nonsense, but just in case you hadn't noticed, people are not the way they *should* be—they *are* the way they *are*.

If you think confronting people is not your style, you are kidding yourself. You confront things day after day. It is not that you don't confront things; maybe you don't confront things in a way that works! It is not a matter of whether confrontation fits your personality; it is not a personality issue at all. You can confront people any way you like—a way that suits your personality. Maybe you can say: "If you want to continue this conversation, you're going to have to talk to me more respectfully," or "I can see you're having a difficult time, and I'm willing to help you, but I'm not helping you by letting you be abusive to me." Think back to times when you handled things well. Be that person again.

It is a matter of learning what works *and* fits your personality. And don't give me that bull about being afraid. Most people have been afraid at one time or another, but have gone on to do what needed to be done anyway. One of my clients called me to tell me she would like to come for an appointment but she was scared. I told her that it was all right to come scared.

When we learn how to walk we fall down sometimes. Have you ever seen a baby try to walk? The baby will be standing there, and for no reason at all, he'll fall down. He'll start walking, then running, and then end up sliding his little face across the carpet. He'll then cry, get up, and try it again. What would happen if he said, "OK, folks, that's it: no more falls for me. I'm scared to get up again, I'm tired of making a fool out of myself, and I'm sick of hearing you giggle when I go down."? A baby keeps on trying.

At what point in our lives do we become so pompous that we don't accept the difficulties of life but want all the rewards? When do we lose the persistence for dealing with life that we were born with? We don't. Our persistence in dealing with life and acceptance for its difficulties are already within us. They're part of our birthright. We just have to reach down deep and pull it out again.

Tools for Confronting Effectively

Put simply, "to confront" means to face or to meet. In order for there to be a confrontation, the other person involved has to know about it. (Otherwise, how could it be a confrontation?) You can confront someone gently with

- humor

- a touch
- a look
- pleasant words

You can confront someone more assertively by

- raising your voice
- looking at him directly
- talking emphatically
- repeating your statement until it sinks in
- expressing your feelings
- standing directly in front of him
- displaying sincere affinity and then being insistent

But *not* effective are

- generalizing
- insulting
- trying to make him feel guilty
- yelling
- threatening
- venting emotion onto him
- being "intense"
- hitting him or throwing something

What follows are some examples of confrontation that may clarify these principles.

There was one husband who would unconsciously block out his wife when in the company of others. If he got involved in a conversation, he would position his body away from her, ignore her, or only half-heartedly attend to what she had to say. She discussed this with him and they agreed that she would touch his arm when he started doing this. In this way, she was able to send him a message without embarrassing him or herself in front of company.

Another way of getting someone to pay attention is to just repeat what you say until it registers. There was another man who came home one evening to a question. His wife asked him if he was going to play cards with his friends that night. She didn't really care if he did or not; she just wanted to know so she could make her own plans. He said, "Can't a guy spend some time with his buddies? I work all week, and I need to spend some time doing what *I* want to do for a change. Can't you understand that?" She said calmly, "Yes, I can. So, are you going to play cards tonight?" He said, "Why are you acting this way?" "Honey," she said, "are you playing cards tonight?" "Yes," he said. "OK," she said, "I'll just go visit with Carol." "Oh," he said.

Still another method for confronting your partner is to first set the tone by saying positive things and getting him to agree with you. And then, once he is agreeing with you and he knows you are generally happy with him, bring up the issue.

She: I know you work hard and you need some time to yourself.

He: Yeah.

She: And did you know it makes *me* feel good when *you* are happy?

He: Yeah?

She: And I think we have a pretty good relationship.

He: So, what are you getting at?

She: (*laughing*) You know me well. I have a big favor to ask.

(*He grows concerned, but he has taken in all the good words.*)

She: It would mean a lot to me if you could get home earlier when you play cards.

He: Like what time?

She: What do you think would be a decent hour? *(Letting him make his own commitment.)*
He: How about one-thirty?
She: *(She had been hoping for one o'clock but she compromises.)* Thanks, honey. See you at one-thirty

Some women will tell you, men are so easy.

Normally, I would not suggest the technique of doing to others what they do to you. In the majority of cases, insulting and judging do not work well. Occasionally, however, if it is done right, done without malice, and not done merely for revenge, it *can* work well. If your guy has good intentions and just doesn't realize how he is affecting you, and if he's come to expect your submission or patience or both, you might try telling him that the next time he lies to you (for example), you are going to lie to him sometime in the future to show him how it feels.

Let me tell you about a woman whose husband verbally abused her. In the heat of an argument, he would purposely say hurtful things. He would yell at her, make threats to dissolve their marriage, insult her, and bring up some of her inadequacies. Later, after he cooled off, he was sorry for having said these things. During one of these cooling off periods, after he said he was sorry, she said, "OK. Well, it seems that your being sorry is not correcting the problem. So, what I am going to do next time this happens is do the same thing you do, so you know how it feels. I won't really mean what I say, but, if you threaten me, I will threaten you. If you insult me, I will insult you, and so forth. This is not negotiable; this *is* what I am going to do—just so you know."

A few weeks later, he came home from work and found that she had left the garage door open. He came in angrily and shouted, "What the hell is the garage door doing open?!" She had barely begun to answer, "I just got home from the market this very minute—" when he started his barrage of verbal abuse. He yelled, "You know, I have some very expensive things in the garage and if someone just walks away with them, *you* can't pay for them because you don't bring home the bacon. I do! You can just sit home on your rear all day, and let me be responsible for everything while you have the girls over for coffee, and then after all that coffee, you have a headache at night and don't want sex. You are so irresponsible, I can't believe it. . . ." She interrupted him by slamming her hand on the table and shouting, "Well, Mr. Macho." (She had his attention then, because she never called him names or made that kind of physical gesture.) She continued in a sarcastic tone, "Since *you* don't want me to work because you want to be the *man* of the house and control your little 'wifey,' I don't have the money to pay for your precious things, but any divorce court will say half of them are mine, anyway. And I do get headaches from having to listen to your crap all night, and besides, I would probably enjoy sex a lot more if your penis was bigger!"

He was flabbergasted.

Then she said sweetly, "I told you I was going to do this, dear. How does it feel?" He finally caught on, and they had a discussion about it. Later that night, he quietly asked, "Do you really think my penis is too small?"

Improving Your Style

Many women already confront their men, but not effectively. They need to learn to modify their confrontations in order to be more productive. If you are telling your partner how to feel, telling him what his attitude is, or telling him what he's thinking, you will have a great margin for error because you can't possibly *know* all these things. Even if you are only 5 he had to find another place to live. She gave him one month to get a job and leave. She had said it before, but he knew she meant it this time. He found a job and an apartment.

I spoke to her recently and asked her if she remembered our last appointment. She sure did. I asked her what had changed. Had she discovered some great technique for living life? She said no, it was just that she now chose things differently, and she found ways to make the things happen, having chosen them. She *chose* not to take on her son's occupational problems, and she gave them back to him to solve. She *chose* to have some recreation in her life and not to take on the problems her husband had with workaholism and thinking spending for vacations was frivolous. She *chose* to work for someone who treated her as an asset instead of a liability. Instead of limiting herself to dealing with her situation, she *chose* a different situation. She had grown enough to see the big picture. Other, better options had been there all the time, just waiting to be *chosen*. After all she had been through, it was just a matter of *choosing* another life.

Another true story:

There were once two women who were good friends. We will call them Mary and Joan. Mary would date only those men who seemed to have their acts together. She wanted each guy to have a good job and to treat her nicely. If her date treated her badly or didn't keep his commitments, she was likely to drop him from her social agenda. She also moved on if she didn't seem to get along well with him.

Joan thought Mary was kind of ruthless. Joan saw the potential in people, and would not refuse a date just because a guy didn't have a job. There were also guys who were moody and abusive, but Joan figured it was probably because they had had bad childhoods, and she didn't hold it against them. Joan felt she could get along with almost anybody.